CLASSIC ENTERTAINING

CLASSIC ENTERTAINING

HENRIETTA SPENCER-CHURCHILL

photography by ANDREAS VON EINSIEDEL

RIZZOLI
NEW YORK

Dedicated to
'SID – AN ERRANT PUBLICAN N.B.'
who knows all about entertaining in style!

First published in the United States of America in 1999 by
Rizzoli International Publications, Inc.
300 Park Avenue South
New York, NY 10010

Copyright © Collins & Brown Limited 1999
Text copyright © Henrietta Spencer-Churchill 1999
Photographs copyright © see copyright holders on page 141

ISBN 0-8478-2182-X
LC 99-70589

Edited by Alison Wormleighton
Designed by Christine Wood
Photography by Andreas von Einsiedel
Photographer's assistant: Philip Harris
Styling by Rose Hammick
Styling on pp 35–9 by Jackie Boase

Reproduction by Hong Kong Graphic & Printing Ltd
Printed and bound in Hong Kong by Imago Services Ltd

Contents

Introduction

To offer food and hospitality is an expression of friendship and community, providing the opportunity to relax and socialize in harmonious surroundings. As a result, for literally thousands of years dining has been surrounded by ceremony and treated almost as an art form. Today, however, because of our hectic lifestyles, dining is being replaced by eating on the run. Yet it is this very pace of life that makes civilized, unhurried meals with friends all the more important – and enjoyable. The purpose of this book is to rekindle that all-important sense of romance, providing both inspiration and practical guidance on stylish entertaining. It is not a step-by-step guide on how to create particular settings, but a comprehensive look at classic entertaining for all occasions, in both historical and contemporary surroundings.

Although many of the photographs show dining rooms, it is certainly not necessary to have a dining room in order to entertain successfully or even to hold formal dinner parties. Because our changing lifestyles have brought new ways of using the space in our homes, the dining room has become an endangered species. If you have one, this book will help you make the most of it; but if you eat in the kitchen or in an open-plan living area instead, you will still be able to adapt most of the ideas from what you see.

I believe strongly that creating the right ambience is the key ingredient when entertaining. You don't have to have a home as grand as those pictured here – it is more important that the setting itself is inviting and atmospheric. As inspiration, I look at a variety of beautiful homes (all photographed specially for it), focusing on how the tables and the rooms have been decorated. The first chapter, Room to Entertain, covers lunch and dinner parties, looking at the room as well as the meal. The second, Creating a Welcome, features other types of entertaining, including breakfasts and brunches, teas, drinks, garden parties and picnics. The third chapter, A Sense of Occasion, covers holiday entertaining, from New Year to Christmas. At the end there is a Directory, which looks at contemporary china, glass, flatware, table linen and other table accessories that can be used to create the classic table.

'Classic' means elegant and timeless, and to many people 'classic entertaining' is based upon the formal dining of the eighteenth century. Sometimes called the Age of Elegance, this was when dining rooms became well-proportioned, symmetrical and supremely elegant, and dining tables began to be laid with beautiful silver, glassware and china. This era provides a superb source of inspiration for formal table settings today, as well as a wealth of useful ideas for less grand occasions. Other periods are also of great interest, in particular the medieval, Elizabethan and Victorian eras, and each is covered, in the context of a home of that period.

Some of the customs that are still in use at formal dinners are delightfully archaic, but etiquette is much less rigid today than it once was. Everyone is more relaxed, and extreme formality seems stuffy and outdated. Nevertheless, classic entertaining entails

Flowers are an important element of a table setting, and, whether I am entertaining in the house or outdoors, formally or informally, I like to use fresh flowers and foliage from the garden.

using your best manners as well as your best tableware, and it is useful to know the correct form, even if you choose not to follow it to the letter. I have therefore included various aspects of etiquette wherever they are relevant.

A beautifully laid table creates a sense of occasion, and here you will find a multitude of inspiring ideas, which can be adapted to any number of guests and to a variety of rooms and occasions, whether formal or informal. Many of the table settings incorporate antique linen, china, glassware or silver, which undoubtedly looks wonderful – but I include as many contemporary pieces as antiques, and I defy you to spot which are old and which are reproduction without reading the captions! We are spoiled for choice these days, and it is perfectly possible to create beautiful classic table settings with no antiques in sight.

I always feel that part of the pleasure of entertaining lies in the planning and preparation, trying out different ideas and then seeing all the elements come together. It is like creating a theatre set in which you determine the mood for the performance of the meal itself. The more care and attention you lavish on your setting, the more

You don't have to have a dining room to give a dinner party – a conservatory or sunroom, a large kitchen, a corner of an open-plan living room or even a large hall can be perfectly suitable.

polished and smooth-running the performance will be. Of course, attempting to be the perfect host can be a daunting business. Not only are you expected to produce a delicious meal, on time, in pleasant and convivial surroundings, but you also have to look after your guests, oil the social wheels – and try to appear calm! Being organized is essential if you are to manage all this, so do as much as possible in advance. Avoid dishes that require much last-minute preparation, as there is nothing less relaxing for your guests than having a host who is constantly in and out of the kitchen. Stick to simple, tried-and-tested recipes. You could even consider buying in ready-made meals which could be served in your own dishes. If you are entertaining a large number of people, ask some friends to help you serve. Most importantly, relax and try to enjoy the occasion yourself. After all, as the librettist W. S. Gilbert said, 'It isn't so much what's on the table that matters as what's on the chairs.'

There is nothing like gleaming silver for creating a sense of occasion. Candles provide the most festive atmosphere at night but usually need to be supplemented by soft background light.

room to
ENTERTAIN

Modern Classic Style

What is the key to successful entertaining? Many different elements come into play, of course, and their relative importance will vary with the occasion and also the people involved. In my view, however, the most important feature is a relaxed and inviting atmosphere.

The welcome must begin at the front door. It may sound obvious, but a well-lit front door or porch – perhaps framed with urns and plants, or dressed with a wreath or garland for special occasions – will immediately set the tone. 'Well lit' does not mean a harsh security light shining in guests' eyes, but soft, subtle lighting with a warm glow, radiating from the entrance hall and drawing the guests in.

Inside the house, it is important that the atmosphere continue. Halls are notoriously stark, utilitarian places, largely because they are treated as passageways rather than rooms in their own right. One of my most important tips as a designer is that all halls, however small, should be treated as liveable rooms. Stone or tiled floors are commonly used here and are perfectly practical and authentic, but they can be cold – not only to the touch but also to the eye. With the simple addition of a rug, the appearance will change and the acoustics of the hall will improve. Wooden floors are visually warmer than stone or tiles, providing a practical surface as well as a richer and cosier atmosphere. Rugs can be used on top of this flooring too, adding even more warmth and colour.

Another instantly welcoming feature, whether it is in the hall, sitting room or dining room, is a log fire. Even on a summer's day it is not unusual to find a lit fire in

an English country house, since the walls of these old buildings are often so thick that the rooms remain cool even when the temperature outside is quite high. And in winter there is nothing more inviting than a crackling log fire. New houses need less warmth than older homes, but an open fire is just as welcoming in a modern house.

The setting for the dinner on these pages is a new house, built in the traditional manner using local stone and set deep in the Oxfordshire countryside. The main staircase hall is entered through a small outer entrance hall, which has a solid front door. A secondary glazed door not only is an attractive architectural feature but also allows natural light to flow into the hall during the day, when the main door can be left open. On this occasion the arched fanlight has been decorated with a garland of

Floor-to-ceiling, wall-to-wall self-pelmeted curtains frame spectacular views, creating a dramatic backdrop for a beautifully laid table.

Top: *An antique linen napkin embroidered with the family's initials is folded and laid on each side plate.*

Above: *The combination of white linen, polished silver, sparkling crystal and blue-and-white bone china gives a crisp, elegant look to the table.*

ivy and berries, tying in with the basket of greenery on the floor, all of which creates a festive atmosphere without being overwhelming.

The dining room is only used at night or for more formal Sunday lunches, as the large family kitchen (shown on pages 64–5) can seat eight to ten people. The two-tone red striped wallpaper in the dining room was chosen with this fact in mind. This is always a good shade for a room that is used principally in artificial light. Not only does it create a warm glow at night, but it is also a good background colour for gilt-framed oil paintings.

The dado and other woodwork have been painted white to give the room a Regency feel, which is enhanced by the simple sisal rug covering the oak-strip floor,

Above: *A late nineteenth-century trailed glass epergne is filled with delphiniums, white roses, a few freesias, bay leaves and trailing ivy and is used for a table centre that subtly echoes the colours of the china.*

and the red and white toile fabric of the curtains. The curtains are most often tied back, allowing the window seats and the door to the terrace to be used as well as making the most of the spectacular views. Plain blinds can be lowered to protect the furnishings from the strong sun and to give privacy at night. The upholstered seats on the dining chairs ensure that diners will be comfortable, however long they linger over their coffee at the end of a meal.

For dinner, a white linen tablecloth covers the traditional Regency mahogany dining table, but for lunch, place-mats are more often used. A late nineteenth-century trailed glass epergne serves as a vase for flowers in the centre of the table.

The table is laid with classic blue-and-white Spode china, which gives a fresh look and provides a nice contrast to the red walls. The use of silverware in a classic pattern and crystal glasses adds formality without looking too grand for the room. A lighthearted touch is the miniature silver basket filled with after-dinner chocolates that decorates each place-setting, once again creating a welcoming atmosphere.

Below left: The Regency sideboard is laid out with cheeses placed on a wooden board lined with laurel leaves. Coffee cups are also set out, as coffee will be taken in the dining room rather than the drawing room in this instance. The glass urns are filled with nougat, and grapes are draped over a glass tazza (a footed, saucer-shaped cup). Like the cheese knife, all of these items look antique but are actually modern.

Below right: An antique Pembroke table provides space on which to display an arrangement, of delphiniums, Moluccella and dyed copper-beech leaves. The after-dinner petits fours are served in Victorian silver baskets, and the silver shell is a serving-spoon warmer.

Opposite: As an alternative to the little silver basket at each place, a small silver candleholder with a red baby candle, echoing the red of the walls, could be set in front of each guest along with his or her place card.

Straight to the point

The cheese knife, like so many other special-purpose implements, was a Victorian invention. It not only has a blade for cutting, but its points allow the cheese to be speared, obviating the need to touch the cheese with the fingers. Unfortunately, many Victorians were unable to resist the temptation to eat the cheese straight from the point of the knife.

A Georgian Dining Room

The dining room featured here has been prepared for both a formal lunch and a formal dinner. The setting is a Queen Anne country house in Northamptonshire. Built between 1702 and 1713 and surrounded by beautiful parkland with lakes and ornamental bridges, the house is thought to have been one of three upon which Jane Austen based Mansfield Park in her novel of that name. Much of the interior was added or changed during the Georgian era, including this dining room. The typical Adam-style plasterwork ceiling, cornice and mantelpiece were installed around 1780, at the time of Robert Adam.

Prior to the eighteenth century, grand dining rooms had not generally existed as separate rooms – a family would eat privately in the parlour or, if entertaining, in the great chamber. However, large-scale entertaining reached new heights during the Georgian era, and the layout of houses was changed in order to accommodate the large numbers of guests. Dining rooms and drawing rooms were of equal size and importance, often symmetrically arranged on either side of the main entrance, as they are in this house. The dining room – which was used only for entertaining, not for family meals – was regarded as the man's domain. This was reflected in the decoration, with fireplaces, plasterwork and pictures depicting hunting or drinking themes. The house featured here has always had close links with both hunting and horse racing, and has a fine collection of sporting paintings, prints and bronzes.

As Georgian dining rooms and entertaining evolved, so did the furniture, which was often specially designed for the room by the architect, such as Robert Adam, or by cabinet-makers of the time like George Hepplewhite and Thomas Sheraton. Dining tables were not a permanent feature of dining rooms; instead, small gateleg tables were set up either individually or together to form one large table, as required. At the end of the century, it became fashionable to have a single enormous mahogany pedestal table, but this was still often dismantled into smaller tables or sections when not in use. Dining chairs lined the walls between meals. In addition, the room would be furnished with one or two mahogany side tables.

As in the room shown here, there would also be an Adam-style mahogany sideboard-table flanked by matching zinc- or lead-lined pedestal cupboards, each displaying a wooden urn (also metal-lined). One of the cupboards was generally used for warming plates and the other for storing wine. Iced drinking water was kept in one urn, and hot water for rinsing glasses and silver cutlery between courses was held in the other. Knives and even chamberpots were also kept in them. Introduced in the

The table is set for a formal dinner party, with a gold-rimmed white china dinner service, along with crystal glasses for white and red wine and water. The arrangement of red roses and snapdragons, palm fronds, golden rod and ivy extends along the centre of the table, and the room is predominantly lit by candlelight, accentuating the warmth of the red scheme.

Opposite top: *A pretty floral centrepiece using flowers from the garden (including pelargoniums, peonies, speedwell and euonymus) adds a touch of femininity to the table, here laid for a formal lunch.*

Opposite bottom left: *The folded napkins contrast attractively with the rounded backs of the upholstered dining chairs.*

Opposite bottom right: *Starched white linen napkins are folded into mitres, lending a neat, structured formality to the place settings.*

1780s, Adam's design became the precursor of the sideboard as we know it today. In the Georgian era it was common to have at least two different dinner services, one for lavish dinner parties and one to use in the daytime and for informal dining. Though lunch was less formal and substantial than dinner, the table still would have been laid on an opulent scale.

For both the lunch and dinner settings featured here we have used the same crystal (including crystal side plates), flatware and candelabras, though the candles would not be lit at a luncheon except for a special occasion such as Christmas. For dinner, although the basics are the same, the table has been dressed up with a more formal flower arrangement and additional silver. With the lit candles providing most of the light, the room takes on a softer, more intimate glow, setting the scene for guests to relax and enjoy themselves.

Above: *An equestrian bronze presides over a set of antique porcelain dessert plates which are used with dessert knives and forks with mother-of-pearl handles. They are laid out on the marble-topped side table ready to serve fruit after the dessert course. All the other china, glassware and silver would be cleared away before this is served.*

21

From hand to mouth

Napkins are now used to dab at lips and fingers, but before the invention of the fork and the toothbrush, they had much more robust functions. They were used for the enthusiastic scrubbing of the teeth after a meal and the wiping of greasy fingers that had been scooping food from a communal pot. A sixteenth-century sage advised, 'It is equally impolite to lick greasy fingers or to wipe them on one's tunic. You should wipe them with the napkin or on the tablecloth.'.

At this time napkins were the size of a bath towel and could almost be confused with the tablecloth: they were supposed to be draped over the left arm or shoulder, like a shawl. By the next century, they were tied around the neck to protect the men's ruffles and lace collars from gravy stains. Towards the beginning of the nineteenth century, napkins found their way to the lap and they have stayed there unobtrusively ever since.

Good lighting is conducive to the enjoyment of good food. An ideal dining room should be flooded with natural light by day so that the lunch table sparkles invitingly with reflections from the silver and glass. By night, nothing can beat the flicker of dancing candlelight. To light the entire room with candles is not really practical, so discreet background lighting is called for. The ambient light in the room should be sufficient for the diners to see what they are eating, and then candles can be used to add atmosphere.

The higher the candle, the more light it sheds, and the taller the candle the more elegant it looks. Short, squat candles are not really appropriate to the formal dinner table, which is the province of the silver candlestick or the candelabra. The flattering glow of candlelight is best shed on the diners from above, or at eye level, as light coming from under the chin casts unwelcome shadows.

Well-polished mahogany, silver and glass all come alive in candlelight, making the formal dinner table inviting and attractive. Even small silver pieces, such as salt cellars, pick up reflections, so it is worth polishing up everything until it shines and placing your silver so that it catches the light. Fine glassware, particularly many-faceted cut glass, has a sparkle that is impossible to copy, and that, too, will be shown off to good advantage by candlelight. Some candelabras, as well as many chandeliers and wall sconces, have glass 'drops' that are designed to maximize the glittering reflections from the light source, and these look beautiful in an appropriate setting.

Opposite: *Contemporary silver shells, each adorned with a single red rose, are used to hold place cards at this formal dinner.*

Right: *Here the table is laid for a weekend lunch party, with a formal look lent by the white table linen and silver accessories. The sporting painting over the fireplace is by Ben Marshall and the other is by George Stubbs.*

Cottage Informality

Left: *The green walls beautifully set off the oak furniture and silver in this dining room. Shown here are a silver punchbowl, pair of candlesticks, candle snuffer, wine taster, sugar shaker and small ornamental pheasant.*

Below: *The dining room of this cottage is typical of rural dining rooms, with its oak country furniture and its table laid for an informal dinner party.*

Hosts and guests often feel more relaxed in a small, intimate dining room such as this one in a low-ceilinged cottage in Oxfordshire. Colour, too, plays a large part in creating a mood, especially at night when candles soften the light and cast interesting shadows. Because the majority of us use our dining rooms mainly at night, strong, bold colours can be used on the walls without worrying too much about the effect during daytime. My particular favourite colours for dining rooms are dark green, reds of all shades, from the oranges to the burgundies, and dark blue. Many people are afraid of using blue, as it has a stigma of being a cold colour, but it can be an excellent background colour for furniture, paintings and collections, particularly as so much porcelain contains blue.

The green paint in this cottage was chosen because it would look good both during the day and at night, as the room is used for a fair number of weekend lunches and dinners. Paint was a more practical option than wallpaper, because the old

limewashed walls were quite rough; it also works better with the stone fireplace and uneven lines of the room.

When selecting furniture for your dining room, consider the style and period of the house as well as the size and proportions of the room. This cottage has low ceilings and oak beams, so oak furniture was more appropriate than mahogany. The table is a typical French-style refectory table. It is antique, but contemporary reproductions in either oak or fruitwood are easy to come by and are perfectly acceptable substitutes. The ladderback chairs, which are also of oak, have rush seats, and these are often used with squab cushions for added comfort. This type of chair, too, is widely available.

The table is laid for an informal dinner party, and the floral dinner service and Biot glassware give a French feel. Using simple white linen place-mats and napkins adds a touch of formality without hiding the beautiful patina of the table. A large bowl of pot-pourri has permanent pride of place as the table centrepiece, and rather than removing it, a pair of candelabra and two fairly low-key arrangements of freesias and bay leaves have been placed on either side. A bowl of fruit or even a sculpture could be treated in a similar way. Another factor in the success of these low-key flowers is the use of three other arrangements around the room. It's not a good idea to have *too* many flowers competing for attention, because the eye doesn't know where to focus, and so these low green and white arrangements are ideal.

Above: *An early twentieth-century cheese knife with a green-dyed ivory handle sits on a contemporary pewter knife rest. Cheese and fruit are often served together, usually after the dessert. At an informal dinner like this, a diner can move his bread plate to the centre of the place-setting to double as a cheese plate.*

Left: *Fresh pale pink garden roses, white freesias and bay leaves are displayed in a silver punchbowl, echoing the rose-patterned fabric of the window-seat cushions and Austrian blinds at the adjacent windows.*

Set pieces

During the eighteenth and nineteenth centuries, rests were supplied so that the same knives and forks could be used from one course to the next, but now we use different ones for each course. The simple rule is to place cutlery in the order in which it is used, working from the outside in, with forks on the left and knives and spoons on the right. So, for the first course, either a small fork is placed on the far left or a soup spoon on the far right. Inside are the fork and knife for the main course, and inside these the dessert fork and spoon. The bread knife, if required, goes either on the far right or on the bread plate at the far left. At informal dinners the dessert fork and spoon are sometimes placed above the plate. At formal dinners they may be brought in with the dessert plates.

Knives were once considered rather risky things to have on the table in case wine-fuelled arguments broke out among guests and the host developed a reputation for keeping an unruly table. However, once a law was passed forbidding sharp points, we learned to live peaceably with the blunt-ended table knife.

A holdover from times when violence at the dinner table was a real threat is the formal dining rule that no more than three knives should be laid at any one place. If more are required to finish off your meal, or your neighbour, they will be supplied by the waiter.

Above: An old jug and matching basin make an ideal vase for a flower arrangement. The pale pink roses, blue and white delphiniums and dyed copper-beech leaves were selected to bring out the colours of the jug.

Right: When not used for serving food, this oak sideboard displays a variety of decorative objects and an informal arrangement of rowan berries and bay. The wooden candlesticks have crowns of berries and ivy, which would be a nice touch for Thanksgiving or Christmas.

Loft Dining

Loft-conversion apartments give a wonderful feeling of light and space, providing a welcome contrast to the cramped, noisy and dirty environment so often associated with large cities. My sister's loft apartment in West London is a good example of this and was the setting for this dinner party for eight. The large, open-plan living area of the apartment is light and airy, with a double-height ceiling and two walls of floor-to-ceiling windows. Instead of curtains, which would have been expensive and claustrophobic, long drops of translucent muslin are simply looped over curtain poles. Some are left flat, so that they pool onto the floor, while others are knotted in the centre. The lengths of blue, rose and reddish-purple muslin, interspersed with white, add rich colour to the room while at the same time enhancing the light, airy atmosphere. At the bottom of the windows, alongside the wood floor, is a channel holding large, smooth pebbles, which add an exotic air.

With the modern, open-plan layout, the exposed brickwork and steel girders, and the collection of Indian and North African textiles and artefacts, the apartment seems an unlikely candidate for a classic table setting. Yet by making colour and light the keynotes, a delightfully flamboyant version of classic style has been produced. The setting is lush and striking yet surprisingly inexpensive to recreate. Although for this occasion some antique glass has been used, it is easy to find contemporary coloured glass at a fraction of the price, and plain fabrics can easily be dyed to match the glass. A white muslin cloth with a subtle self-stripe has been laid over the wooden refectory

Left: *This exotic table setting was influenced by the strong colours of the muslin window hangings and by the overall theme of the loft apartment, which is an eclectic mix of Morocco and the East.*

Right: *A simple painted tray is set ready for pre-dinner drinks with an assortment of contemporary St Louis tumblers and glasses.*

table, and a runner of fuchsia-pink muslin breaks this up. The white linen napkins, with a tiny piece of mirror appliquéd onto each, come from India, while gold damask napkins folded in half twice have become elegant table-mats. The chairs are surprisingly simple, but, because of that, do not detract from the table setting. For a more exotic feel, however, they could be covered with simple slipcovers of neutral or coloured cotton.

Candlelight is an essential part of a dinner setting, and a room of this height demands tall, elegant candelabra. These Gothic-revival ormolu (gilded) candelabra, c.1835, are ideal in terms of both finish and stature, and work well with the gold rims on the glasses. For a less grand and cheaper alternative, large wooden candlesticks with church candles could be used.

Following the exotic theme, rather than having the more traditional type of floral centrepiece, two potted orchids have been removed from their pots and set in an early twentieth-century rose-coloured glass vase by Moser. Large pebbles taken from the

Rights and wrongs

At formal dinners a plate of food is presented from the diner's right and the empty plate is removed from the left. When dishes are brought to guests for them to serve themselves, however, the dishes are presented from the left. Wineglasses are filled from the right. Port is always passed to the guest of honour (who is seated to the right of the host), or poured for them by the host, and then it is passed to the left (clockwise) around the table, with the guests serving themselves.

Left: *Although the table and chairs are very simple, the use of coloured glass and a mixture of silver and gilt adds a rich, exotic feel to this table setting.*

Opposite: *These spectacular contemporary coloured hock glasses and champagne flutes with gold decoration would make any pre-dinner drinks very special.*

collection under the windows cover the soil and moss and provide another visual link with the apartment. They are flanked by two pineapples, and the result is an arrangement that is tall enough to stand up (quite literally) to the splendid candelabra and the height of the room without obstructing the sight lines of guests.

The real key to this sparkling look is the glassware. Even the plates, which are American, c.1910, are glass, inlaid and monogrammed with silver. These are echoed by the silver-rimmed glass coasters. The cranberry-coloured wineglasses are modern reproductions, while the exquisite gold-banded, coloured-glass tumblers are inexpensive Moroccan mint-tea glasses. Like the table linen, the colours of the glassware, including even the mineral water bottles, pick up those of the muslin curtains. For the wine connoisseur, wishing to check wine colour and clarity, coloured glass may not be the best choice, but for cocktails and water, it is highly decorative.

Opposite top: *Moroccan mint-tea glasses in two sizes and reproduction cranberry-coloured hock glasses add glorious splashes of colour to the dining table.*

Opposite bottom: *The beauty of an open-plan living area is that the entire space can be utilized by dinner guests, making a dinner party very relaxed.*

Another light touch in the table setting is provided by the mother-of-pearl salt and pepper pots, spoons and shell-dishes, which could perhaps be used for butter pats. Mother-of-pearl handles on the flatware extend the theme and look particularly pretty with the glass plates.

One of the big attractions of an open-plan living area like this is that it is perfect for entertaining. Conversations do not have to be curtailed while everyone makes their way to and from the dining room, since drinks and after-dinner coffee are served in the same room as the meal. Nor does the cook miss out on the conversation, since the kitchen is separated from the rest of the room only by a breakfast bar. Siting the main seating area at one end of the room leaves plenty of space at the other end not just for the dining area but for friends and family to gather, and also for smaller, more intimate seating groups, all of which add to the relaxed atmosphere.

Below: *A corner is furnished with bamboo chairs and a wood-and-cane settee, Indonesian in style, providing a conversation area away from the main seating. The subtle colours of the walls contrast with the bright muslin without detracting from the artwork on the walls. The use of natural materials like wood, plants and stones gives this loft a feeling of the outdoors.*

Sumptuous Surroundings

Set in a beautiful park in Oxfordshire, the country house that is the setting for the lunch and dinner pictured on these pages has a long history as a royal hunting lodge. Although parts of the house date back to the sixteenth century, most of the architecture is of the seventeenth century. The dining room is predominantly late nineteenth-century but in the Georgian-revival style. It is typically used either for winter shooting lunches (as on pages 34–7) or for more formal dinners (as on pages 38–9). Although the lunch is a fairly informal occasion, the fact that the dining room is quite grand naturally dictates a more formal table setting.

What I love about this table is its size and stature, in particular the width, as it allows space for lavish table centres and many silver accoutrements. During the eighteenth century, when the food was placed on large platters in the centre of the table (which was known as service *à la française*) – rather than served individually (which was called service *à la russe*), as it was from the nineteenth century onwards – it was beneficial to have wide tables.

As well as masses of food, the table often would hold an elaborate centrepiece consisting of a miniature landscape, garden or architectural feature constructed from sugar, dough and wax and laid on a mirrored plate. This was the origin of the centrepieces we know today, although fresh flowers were not fashionable at this time; it was the artificiality of the centrepiece that was appreciated.

Dinner was the main meal and the focal point of the day. At the beginning of the Georgian period it was served at around midday, but gradually the fashionable dinner hour became later and later. By the early nineteenth century it was being served at about seven o'clock.

Dinner guests, in full evening dress, would gather in the drawing room and then file into the dining room when dinner was announced. It was typical for men and women to sit at opposite ends of the table (although the end of the Georgian period saw the introduction of so-called 'promiscuous seating', in which men and women sat alternately). In grand houses like the one pictured here, the meal, which consisted of

Above: *Don't hesitate to experiment with centrepieces. Here, hyacinths and* Ononis fruticosa *surround the base of each of the fragrant standard rosemary trees in baskets on the table.*

Opposite: *Because the dining room is often used for shooting lunches, as here, as well as more formal dinners, the large mahogany dining table is always kept at full size. For this lunch, the table is left exposed and white lace place-mats are used.*

A pinch of salt

Salt has always been treated with respect. A large salt cellar (from the French 'sel', for salt) used to be placed near the lord of the manor and his most important guests: anyone of less status sat 'below the salt'. Today, at a formal dinner in Britain and on the Continent, a cellar is placed in front of every diner. If there is no salt spoon, it is acceptable to take a pinch of salt with one's fingers, since nobody else is using that particular cellar. Salt is placed in a little heap on the plate – at formal dinners sprinkling it from a salt shaker is still not quite proper.

Opposite, clockwise from top left:
The old Irish linen napkins, embroidered with the family crest, are folded simply and laid on the side plates.

The dinner service was custom-designed to incorporate the family crest. With its white ground and blue and gilt border, it is suitable for both day and evening use.

A whole Stilton cheese surrounded by grapes and strawberries provides an additional table decoration. Cheese is generally served after dessert, with a glass of port or sloe gin.

Here, salt cellars are paired with ivory pepper mills, also bearing the family's crest.

two or three courses served by a large retinue of servants, would last for several hours. At the end of the meal, everything was removed (or 'de-served', which is the origin of the word dessert), including the tablecloth and napkins, and dishes of fruit and sweetmeats were brought in. The meal tended to become less formal at this point, and the men and women might sit together.

Below: A wide dining table does make conversing across the table a little more difficult, but the size and shape of a table should be in keeping with the scale of the room. This large, rectangular room demands a good-sized, oblong table. A square room would look best with a round table, which could perhaps be extended with leaves to a small oval.

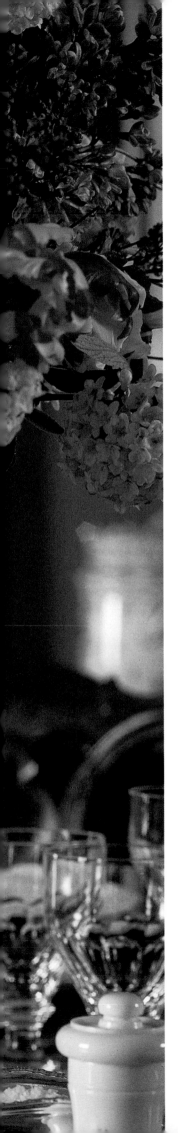

Above: *The chandelier and candelabras provide a softer light for this dinner setting. Although the linen, china and silver have not been changed from lunchtime, there are now two wineglasses, for each guest.*

Left: *The flowers used for the dinner setting – white and purple lilacs, parrot tulips and viburnum – are in colours that tie in with the overall decoration and are more delicate and feminine than the rosemary trees used for the luncheon table.*

Following the sweetmeats, the ladies would retire to the drawing room – originally known as the withdrawing room – to play cards, sew and drink tea. The servants were sent away, and the gentlemen were left to smoke, drink wine and port, and discuss politics. Seating hierarchies were abandoned at this stage; the men could sit where they liked. After an hour or more, the men would join the ladies for tea, cards, music, conversation and perhaps dancing. Eventually, at the end of the evening, an informal supper might be served in the dining room or another room.

Although luncheon was only a light snack early in the century, it became increasingly substantial as the dinner hour got later (and breakfasts earlier), and by the early nineteenth century it had become a proper sit-down meal in the middle of the day. For either meal, the dining table was covered with a white linen cloth, with matching napkins, and laid with bone china, silver and glassware.

For both the luncheon and the dinner featured here, white table-mats and napkins bearing the family crest enhance the fine china and the silverware, which also bear the family crest. At night, with the curtains closed, the candlelight reflecting off the crystal, sculpted silver centrepiece and ormolu (gilt) candelabras creates an atmospheric and memorable dinner.

Understated Elegance

The setting for this dinner for eight is a rambling seventeenth-century stone farmhouse set in the Wiltshire countryside. Elements of the house – some fifteenth-century stone arches, windows and a fireplace – were taken from an earlier house that was on the site, while Georgian windows were added in the eighteenth century. Its beautiful, unspoilt setting makes the house seem like a romantic hideaway, and, in fact, it was used as Grace Melbury's home in a recent film of Thomas Hardy's novel *The Woodlanders*.

The dining room, which used to be the morning room, has the feel of a Georgian parlour that would have been used by the family for informal dining when not entertaining guests. The dado was added by the present owners and painted in a traditional Georgian single tone of pale green. The built-in storage cupboards on either side of the fireplace are mahogany but the owners painted them in the same green to tie in with the rest of the woodwork and make the room brighter. The glass-fronted doors are backed by Indian sari fabric, while the bottom of each cupboard is open and holds logs. The grey marble fire surround was also painted, in an off-white tone, so that the contrast with the walls was not so great. Above each cupboard, the wall was hand-painted in a trailing leaf design to give the effect of a pediment.

The colour scheme for this room works well both during the day and at night. In the daytime it is light and airy, and the sunlight filters through the lightweight embroidered curtains that hang on a pole hand-painted to match the woodwork. At night, the warm glow of the candlelight and the light from the open fire are reflected in the pale walls.

Above the fireplace sits a traditional, simple overmantel which has a silver gilt finish rather than the more common gold colour. In dining rooms, mirrors were often placed over fireplaces so as to reflect the light from the candelabras and candle-burning chandeliers.

The floor is wooden, a practical choice for a room where meals are taken. It was originally a dark colour but the original boards have been sanded down, leaving a natural, lighter oak finish. A rug adds warmth and colour to the room as well as absorbing some of the sound.

Because of its shape and generous width, the mahogany dining table can accommodate two place-settings at each end, although the diners will be slightly constricted. To make sure that everyone seated at a table has enough elbow room, it is advisable to allow at least 60 centimetres (2 feet) for each place-setting. This also ensures that there is room on the table for all the necessary plates, flatware and glassware, as well as serving dishes, salt cellars and other accoutrements, which sometimes need to be placed between diners as well as in the centre.

Interestingly, three different styles of chair are used at the table, which in my opinion is perfectly acceptable, as they are of a similar period, style and wood. In fact,

Above: *A garland of fresh hops, hydrangea and asters, contrasting beautifully with the stone of the farmhouse, creates a warm welcome at the front door.*

Opposite: *This fresh and light dining room provides a simple yet elegant atmosphere for a dinner party.*

Below: *A single colour of hydrangea, with* Euphorbia marginata, *has been used to decorate an antique silverplated epergne, acting as a pretty table centre.*

Right: *A collection of antique lead-crystal decanters and glasses forms a display on a mahogany sideboard. The decanters are traditionally used for serving red wine, port and sherry. The small oil painting is by Herring and is typical of the type of sporting paintings found in country dining rooms.*

Below: *These attractive contemporary wineglasses are engraved with vine leaves and grapes. Drinking themes and motifs are often found in architectural details such as plaster cornices or fireplaces in dining rooms.*

in my own country house I use two different sets of four side chairs along with a contrasting pair of carvers.

To buy an original set of ten to twelve period dining chairs can be expensive, let alone trying to find ones that you like which are comfortable, so mixing sets is a practical alternative. Another solution is to buy a smaller set of chairs in a style that you like, and then have the rest copied from these. A good cabinetmaker can produce excellent copies with enough distressing of the wood that even you may not be able to tell them from the originals!

The table setting is deliberately simple, yet elegant, to complement the overall ambience of the room. Underplates have been used instead of table-mats or a tablecloth. These are antique Minton and are part of the dinner service, but it is quite common to use a contrasting underplate, which could be in silver, pewter, brass, glass or, for grander settings, gilt. To protect the surface of the table from hot plates, it may be sensible to use small, round mats, perhaps of cork, beneath the underplates.

Silver flatware, candlesticks and cruets add a certain formality to the table. For a lunch setting, these would probably be replaced with bone- or ivory-handled stainless

Below: *Made in a contemporary light crewelwork fabric and held back with silver ribbons, the curtains are kept simple to continue the theme of a Georgian parlour.*

steel flatware, wooden accoutrements and plain glass. The simple flower arrangement adds a necessary splash of colour and height yet does not detract from the delicate design of the china. The vase is an Edwardian silverplated epergne – a silver or glass centrepiece consisting of several shallow dishes supported on branches, which was used from the eighteenth to the early twentieth centuries to hold sweetmeats, fruits, condiments or, later, flowers, as here. Floral foam is used to hold the flowers securely in place in the dishes.

To create a special welcome for guests, the thick, studded oak front door and stone arch has been dressed with a garland made from pre-twisted lengths of fresh hops and branches of hydrangea. Supported by two wooden washing-line props hidden in the foliage, the garland looks almost as though it were growing around the door.

Below: *Individual pieces of porcelain and glass can be combined to form an attractive display ideally suited to a dining room. Here, in front of a ceramic vase, an assortment of glass eggcups, bowls and an underplate in glorious colours glistens in the light from a nearby window.*

Bottom left: The mantelshelf provides a display area for Georgian 'Bristol green' decanters and gilt-decorated goblets, all late eighteenth century. The cherub vases hold greenery and flowers from the garden, and the whole display is reflected in the silver painted overmantel.

Below left: A pretty set of antique mocha cups is displayed in its original case. The silver and enamel coffee spoons are contemporary.

Below right: Japanese anemones float in late Victorian gold-rimmed finger-bowls.

The ornamental finger-bowl

Pretty additions to the dining table, finger-bowls look particularly attractive with flowers floating in them. However, their origins are much less refined, as they are a relic of the days when people ate their meals largely with their fingers. In the past a diner might dip his napkin into the finger-bowl and wipe his mouth and chin, or even rinse out his mouth with the water from the finger-bowl and then spit into it. Today, a finger-bowl is used for fingertips only, which are then dried daintily on the napkin in one's lap. Finger-bowls are particularly welcome if whole artichokes, shellfish or asparagus is on the menu. At very formal dinners, they are brought in on the dessert plates with the dessert knives and forks.

A Historic Setting

In a home like this, where you feel history all around you, one approach to entertaining is to go for a historical treatment. This stone manor house in Dorset is principally Elizabethan, although parts of it date back to medieval times. The dining room, pictured here, was rebuilt in the late sixteenth century, and the oak wainscot panelling, plaster overmantel and high moulded-plaster ceiling are all from that time. Central heating has not been installed, and so the fires heat the rooms just as they have for centuries. There is electricity, however, whereas in Elizabethan times the only lighting would have been from candles. The furniture is mainly seventeenth-century oak and includes a refectory table, rush-seated chairs, a court-cupboard and several serving tables and buffets.

In Elizabethan times there might have been paintings, tapestries or other textiles hanging on the walls above the half-panelling, but there would have been no rug on the floor. Rugs were reserved for tables, window seats or beds. Instead, the floorboards might have been covered with rush matting or loose rushes.

At mealtimes, the family and guests would sit around an oak refectory table similar to this one. The master, mistress and important guests would be seated upon oak chairs, while the children and less important guests would sit on stools. Cushions were used on the chairs to make them a little more comfortable. A white cloth would be laid over the table and its table carpet, and then napkins, ornamental cups and 'salts' placed on top.

Wealthy households ate from silver, gold or pewter plates and dishes and drank from Venetian glasses and silver tankards. The family might own many pewter items, including candlesticks, tureens, salvers and chargers (large, flat dishes), plates, salts and cruets, spoons, mugs, tankards, jugs and flagons (lidded jugs). Food was served on large platters and dishes, similar to the ones seen here, and placed in the centre of the table, after the meat had been carved ceremoniously. Ewers of water and napkins were provided for washing drinking vessels, utensils and hands before a meal and between courses – an important ritual since much of the food was eaten by hand.

Dinner was eaten at around midday, and the duration of the meal was dependent upon whether guests were present. It was typical for two main courses to be served for everyday dining, but when guests were being entertained it could extend to three or more courses and last for many hours, with entertainment between courses. Guests helped themselves to any dishes they could reach, and servants would serve them to any other dishes they wanted. The food was generally washed down with ale, beer, cider

This Elizabethan room is furnished with the traditional pieces of oak furniture and predominantly pewter accessories used at that time. The oak refectory table is laden with pieces that would have been used for eating and serving food, in both modern and antique pewter. The spiky globe-artichoke flowers in the jug on the table suit the unfussy, robust style of the room.

or wine, as water was unsafe, and tea and coffee didn't arrive until over a century later. Because the Elizabethans were fond of music, guests might be asked to play the lute or recorder after the table had been cleared. In grand homes, minstrels might play in a minstrels' gallery.

To take inspiration from a historical setting like this one, I am not suggesting that you go to extremes and try to recreate an authentic Elizabethan evening! But your table decoration should complement the room's architecture and furnishings. In this room, the clear choice is pewter, a selection of which is shown in the process of being laid out. Glass plates will be used on top of the pewter underplates. These underplates are modern, like much of the other pewter on the table. Because pewter items that are inexpensive but of good quality are still manufactured today, it is not necessary to own a massive collection of valuable antique pieces to create this Elizabethan look.

For a less spartan, more elegant effect, silver or gold and cut glass could be used instead of pewter. They look sumptuous against dark oak (as in the picture opposite) and can be mixed freely with older and newer items (as pictured below). It is good to be sensitive to the historical context of the surroundings but at the same time have confidence in your own eye. In any period house, knowing what originally would have been used in the dining room, or in any room, will make you more discerning in your choices, but ultimately you have to go for the look that you intuitively feel is right. This will help ensure that the table setting matches not just the room but also the occasion and your own personal style.

Below left: A seventeenth-century oak side table displays an eclectic combination of antique pewter candlesticks, Georgian silver and nineteenth-century decanters. The eucalyptus, ivy, viburnum and sea holly are held in modern wrought iron candlesticks with floral foam.

Below right: Cut-glass decanters filled with port, claret and sherry sit in silver wine coasters, which can also be used on tables for wine bottles. Cut-glass decanters, with their silver labels and coasters, did not appear till the end of the eighteenth century but they still look superb in this earlier setting.

Opposite: These elegant gold-rimmed cut-glass goblets with hexagonal bases were made by Moser in the early twentieth century and look wonderful against the background of the oak court-cupboard.

Above: A simple pewter
tankard has been used as a
vase for hydrangea, sea
holly and laurel, and
contrasts nicely with the
heavy and elaborately
carved wooden fireplace.

Cut and thrust

Early cutlery was very basic and was only provided to important guests – others
brought their own cutlery with them, a practice which lasted until the end of the
eighteenth century. Knives were used for taking pieces of food from a platter and
cutting it up, but the food was actually eaten with the fingers, except for liquid and
semi-liquid foods, which were eaten with spoons.

Forks were only used for eating sticky desserts. In the seventeenth century, people
began to use forks but would often share them, considerately wiping them on a
napkin before passing them on. Perhaps this is the reason that the English and
Americans continued to prefer using their fingers, long after the Europeans
had adopted forks.

By the nineteenth century, the custom in Britain, Europe and America was to
cut one piece of food holding the fork in the left hand and the knife in the right,
then lay down the knife and transfer the fork to the right hand before taking the
piece of food to the mouth. Late in that century, however, the English began lifting
the food to the mouth on the back of the fork using the left hand, with the knife still
held in the right – a practice previously thought very coarse. The procedure was
copied in Europe but was resisted in North America, where the previous practice
is still followed to this day.

Opposite: Antique white
table linen sets off the
deep, rich grey of the
pewter and is also
historically correct. The
cutlery and flagon are
antique, while the napkin
rings are modern.

50

Entertaining under Glass

A conservatory or sunroom is a versatile addition to either a country house or a town house, simultaneously providing extra living space and an all-weather garden – and is an invaluable spot for entertaining. The conservatory in which the lunch pictured on these pages is set is in the grounds of a Dorset country house. Although it is not attached to the house, it is frequently used for family meals and entertaining. It was built only ten years ago, but replicates a dilapidated conservatory formerly on the site.

Plants are the *raison d'être* of a conservatory, and strategically planted climbers and large feature plants not only provide shade but help blur the distinction between indoors and out. Against this permanent background can be set a changing display of hanging baskets and potted plants. This was the approach taken in the nineteenth and early twentieth centuries, when hanging baskets, freestanding ceramic jardinières and wirework plant-holders filled with pots of plants were set against a background of ferns and tall plants. Even in the eighteenth century, when orangeries and conservatories were first developed to protect exotic plants brought back by travellers, the container-grown orange trees and other plants would be taken out and placed on the terrace in the spring, and the space inside was then occasionally used for entertaining.

Because the conservatory featured here is long and relatively narrow, the space automatically splits up into two areas. At one end is a small plunge pool and at the other a fountain, which feeds the pool through a channel running down the centre of the terracotta floor and covered by an iron grille. A long, narrow wooden table, which seats ten on cushioned wrought iron chairs, takes pride of place near the fountain. For the informal weekend lunch pictured here, the table has been laid with an antique French tablecloth with matching napkins. Plain white china, silver flatware and green-tinted glasses keep the look simple.

Left: The conservatory is set up for an informal weekend lunch using a simple wooden table covered with an antique French cloth. The wrought iron chairs with their striped cotton cushions are perfect for the room. My one basic rule for furnishing conservatories is to keep them natural, as close to the outdoors as possible. In other words, stick to wood, rattan, bamboo or metal furniture with plain, striped or checked fabrics, and avoid curtains and upholstered furniture.

Right: Two verdigris candelabras hold an informal arrangement of Sorbus berries and foliage. When combining floral material and lit candles, it is important never to leave them unattended.

Although there are no blinds to provide shade in the heat of the day, the sunlight is filtered through a venerable grapevine clambering up the wall and across the ceiling, as well as palms and other large plants. The dappled shade and sound of running water create an idyllic spot for long, relaxed lunches. Climbing plants growing up trellising on one long, windowless wall add to the verdant greenery surrounding the diners.

The space is also often used for entertaining at night. Lighting a conservatory at night-time can be tricky, because the enormous expanse of glass becomes black and forbidding. However, soft lighting such as twinkly low-voltage halogen lights, night-lights in jars, lanterns and a multitude of candles produces atmospheric reflections in the glass. Lighting concealed among the plants also creates magical effects.

A place of one's own

At a formal dinner, or in a grand restaurant, a 'place' is a personal space not to be trespassed upon. It is delineated by its flatware and filled with an underplate, also called a 'service plate', or in some instances by a napkin, so that the place is never empty and therefore inviting intrusion. Underplates are not used for eating, merely for decoration.

Opposite top: *A few wicker chairs are scattered around the pool at the other end of the conservatory from the table, providing a pleasant area for pre-lunch drinks or coffee after a meal.*

Opposite bottom left: *Each place is laid with a simple white china underplate, dinner plate and soup bowl, and a wine glass and water goblet.*

Opposite bottom right: *The beautiful old linen napkins have been embroidered with the owner's initials.*

Right: *Large plants including palms and a well-established grapevine provide dappled shade for the table, which sits next to a lion's-head fountain.*

55

Above: *The magnificent wood-panelled double doors into the dining room of the château are picked out in gilt. The carvings represent both Diane de Poitiers and Henri II, and the hunt for which she was famed.*

Left: *With its rich combination of wood panelling and tapestries, the French Renaissance dining room oozes warmth. The giltwood chandelier is a nineteenth-century copy of an earlier one.*

Dinner at a Château

Cooking and eating are two of life's greatest pleasures for the French. Meals have always been social occasions in France, and no book on classic entertaining would be complete without some acknowledgement of the French contribution. Consequently, I have included here a dining room in a French château, belonging to cousins of mine on my mother's side.

The Château d'Anet, in Normandy, is steeped in romantic history, but is most remembered as being the home of Diane de Poitiers, the mistress of Henri II, twenty years her junior, who came to the throne in 1547 following the death of his father, François I. Although there have been châteaux on the site since the twelfth century, the present building dates back to 1547, when Diane commissioned the architect Philibert de l'Orme to replace the previous Gothic manor with an imposing classic-revival masterpiece. Diane died at the château in 1566.

Throughout the next hundred years, it remained relatively unchanged, although in a poor state of repair, and then in the late seventeenth century it was modernized. The château was once regarded as the finest of all French Renaissance châteaux, but much of the original building was destroyed in 1804; what remained was renovated in the nineteenth century. Today, the château, which is open to the public (and is pictured on page 76), is acknowledged as an important historical monument. Restoration continues, and many of the original works of art associated with the house have been returned. The interior has many references to Diane de Poitiers that conjure up poignant images of her life there.

The dining room is not a large room. With its wood panelling and the hunting themes depicted in the tapestries, it is typically masculine in feel. The fireplace is an impressive focal point, with two walnut figures carved by Pierre Puget supporting the mantelpiece that carries Diane's coat of arms. The inscription on the frieze is from Virgil and was taken from the original sixteenth-century dining room. It reads: '*dapibus mensas oneramus inemptis*', which translates as 'our tables are laden with viands which are not bought'.

The table is laid for an intimate dinner for eight – not overly grand but formal enough to live up to the surroundings. The focal point of the table, which is covered in a heavy damask cloth and damask table-mats, is a beautiful Dutch Renaissance silver ship centrepiece. The dinner plates, which are late seventeenth-century, are from Vieux Rouen, while the wineglasses date from the early eighteenth century. The

Right: *Hung on one side of the fireplace, this tapestry is part of a series in the room depicting bear and duck hunting and falconry. Hunting and falconry were popular with both Diane and Henri. The candelabras are Dutch Renaissance.*

Below: *This magnificent silver ship is Dutch Renaissance and was originally used to roll wine decanters along the length of the table. Today it serves as an impressive decorative centrepiece.*

story goes that the glasses were modelled on the breasts of Diane de Poitiers! Whether this is true or not, the whole room is a great testimony to an unusual woman, whose strong presence and influence can still be felt throughout the château.

Taking a seat

It is the custom in England and North America for the host and hostess to sit at the ends of the table, with their respective guests of honour next to them, as the ends are the most visible and therefore important positions. But in France and some other European countries, the centre is the hallowed territory. The host and hostess sit opposite each other in the middle of the long sides, and the least important guests are banished to the table's ends.

The customs of splitting up couples at the table and of alternating men and women around the table are still followed fairly scrupulously. For dinner parties seating multiples of four, however – like this one, set for eight – the hostess has to relinquish the end seat in order to preserve the man–woman sequence.

Left: The table is set with a rich damask cloth and contrasting damask place-mats for an intimate dinner. The soft light from the candles on the side table and from the chandelier adds to the feeling of intimacy. The flowers, which have been used on the side tables as well as on the dining table, are golden rod, chrysanthemums, gypsophila, sea lavender, foam flower and ferns.

Above right: *This silver lady is a Dutch wedding cup, dating from 1560. The smaller, upper cup swivels and was meant to be used by the wife, while the larger, base cup was designed for the husband. It is now used as a bell.*

Above far right: *The centre motif of the late seventeenth-century Vieux Rouen dinner plates depicts 'la corne d'abondance', signifying wealth and prosperity. The size of the symbol, a well-known motif from the Vieux Rouen factory, is an indication of the date.*

Right: *An original Renaissance wine decanter is decorated with symbols representing Diane and Henri. The crescents are her symbols, the fleurs-de-lys represent him, while the entwined 'D' and 'H' symbolize the pair.*

creating a WELCOME

Casual Breakfast or Brunch

An invitation to someone's kitchen for a meal was once a sign of intimacy, but today even large dinner parties are often held in the kitchen. And if you have people staying for the weekend, breakfast or brunch is more than likely to be served there. In fact, brunch is also a nice way to entertain guests who are not staying with you. A happy combination of breakfast and lunch, it is perfectly suited to a lazy Sunday morning.

Neither breakfast nor brunch *has* to be served in the kitchen, of course, but if you have a family kitchen it is tailor-made for this sort of entertaining. Many homes have farmhouse-style kitchens complete with a small sofa, a large table and an Aga cooking range. I have always yearned for an Aga, as it not only gives the room a focal point but also provides additional warmth on cold, wintry days.

To entertain successfully in the kitchen, you need appropriate lighting – not just good general lighting and task lighting in the work area, but more atmospheric lighting in the dining area for evening meals. If the table is also used for homework and other jobs, you could satisfy both criteria with a pendant light on a dimmer switch. Having it on a separate circuit allows you to switch off the lights illuminating the dirty pots and pans. If your kitchen chairs are wooden, tie-on cushions will make them more comfortable.

Many tables are in the middle of the kitchen, as here, which makes them handy as a work surface. But you do have to accept that cooking detritus will be in full view, and that you will be cooking right next to your seated guests. If the eating area is at one end of the room, on the other hand, it may be possible to hide the sink and preparation area from view with a cupboard or breakfast bar.

The table here, which is in the same house as the dining room featured on pages 12–17, has been set for an informal weekend breakfast. Everyone can appear at different times and help themselves to juice, fruit, cereals, breads and toast, boiled eggs, coffee and tea. For a brunch, which is served in the late morning instead of breakfast or lunch, you could provide all of this plus bagels, muffins, croissants or Danish pastries, and perhaps scrambled eggs with smoked salmon. Plenty of luscious fruit is essential for a brunch menu, while drinks such as Bucks Fizz (also known as a Mimosa – freshly squeezed orange juice with champagne) and Bloody Mary (tomato juice and vodka) are optional extras.

Breaking bread

A slice of bread or bread roll is supposed to be broken (not cut) into bite-sized pieces, rather than being bitten and put back down on the table or side plate. Our aversion to the sight of teeth-marks in 'abandoned' pieces of food probably goes back to medieval times and the communal bowl.

This large table can seat up to ten people and is often used for informal meals with family and friends. The Aga cooking range ensures that the kitchen will be warm at all times.

Lakeside Celebration

On a lovely summer's day there is no nicer way to entertain than out in the garden. Whether you have a walled garden in a city or a rambling garden in the country, out of doors is where everyone will want to be. The occasion may be a celebration, such as a christening, birthday or anniversary, or you may simply have invited friends for drinks or a light meal – but whatever the occasion, everything tastes better outside.

The garden party pictured here was by a lake in the grounds of the country estate featured on pages 18–23, while the table with champagne was set up in the formal gardens near the house. I decide which part of my garden to use for a party according to the time of year and also the time of day, so that it is in full bloom and in the best possible light.

At midday, shade should be available, whether in the form of trees, a pergola or a marquee or tent. A large marquee is also useful if you are entertaining a lot of people and cannot rely on the weather. The tent shown here is only big enough to cover a small table, but its styling makes it very romantic and appropriate to period surroundings.

Existing garden furniture can obviously be used, particularly if you have the type of table that can be extended. However, it is an easy matter to cover a couple of card tables with tablecloths and accessories. I prefer to use simple checks and stripes, rather

Left: *A marquee or tent provides a focal point for a garden party – and a sense of occasion. This one is in the style of tents used by the British Raj in nineteenth-century India.*

Below: *A garden bursting with flowers provides a splendid setting for entertaining friends.*

Below left: Flowers make any table look more special, even in the garden. Here I have used a selection of flowers, berries and foliage from the garden. The quails' eggs are held in an antique glass tazza.

Below right (top): A modern Aubusson rug and a grey cashmere throw add touches of sheer luxury.

than floral fabrics which may compete with the surroundings. Crisp antique linens in white or neutral colours look equally stylish.

For an informal lunch I prefer Pimms with lots of fruit to champagne, but champagne or a crisp, dry white wine, well chilled, makes a perfect start to an evening. It is, of course, polite to offer alternatives such as spirits and soft drinks, and canapés. Being outdoors gives you plenty of freedom with the presentation of canapés, and I use wooden platters or baskets lined with natural foliage or checked linen napkins.

The vulgar fish knife

Silver fish knives and forks were a Victorian invention, along with sardine forks, jelly knives, tomato servers and cheese scoops. However, they were considered unspeakably middle-class by the aristocracy, as owning a set was a sure sign that one had recently purchased the family silver instead of having inherited it.

Opposite: A large leaf and a pewter underplate at each place set off the etched glass plates and luscious summer fruit. All the tableware shown here is contemporary, apart from the c.1910 agate-handled gold cutlery.

Below right (bottom): The contemporary gold-embroidered organza tablecloth comes from India and, like the tent, evokes British hill stations in the days of the Raj.

Country House Breakfast

There is nothing more comforting when waking up on a cold, wintry morning in the countryside, than to be greeted with a traditional cooked breakfast. This is all the more welcome if you are staying at an old country house, as these are known for their lack of heating. The setting for this breakfast is the dining room of a Worcestershire country house dating back to medieval times. The Gothic-style windows overlook a half-timbered courtyard, which was created in the nineteenth century.

In medieval and Tudor times breakfast was, for the upper classes, quite a substantial meal. It consisted of a variety of breads, cold meats, saltfish and cheese, and was served with ale or wine, as coffee and tea had not yet been introduced. An informal occasion, it was often served in the privacy of the bedchamber at between six and seven o'clock in the morning. This custom continued until the end of the seventeenth century, when the continental-style breakfast became fashionable among the wealthy. It consisted of a lighter meal of breads and cakes served with hot tea, coffee and milk at around nine or ten in the morning.

The 'breakfast party', introduced at the end of the eighteenth century, became a popular new way of entertaining large groups of people. The guests would be served cold food and would listen to music and stroll around the house and grounds. During

Right: *The view through Gothic-style windows to a half-timbered courtyard provides a splendid backdrop for this informally laid buffet. Guests can select from a variety of continental pastries and cooked dishes kept warm in silver tureens.*

Below: *A traditional country-house breakfast is laid out on an oak refectory table which acts as a sideboard here.*

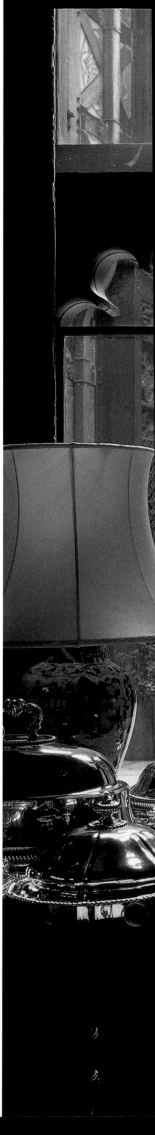

the nineteenth century these parties got later and later, until they became the afternoon garden parties we are familiar with today.

The Victorians regarded eating as a social necessity, and during the early part of the nineteenth century, breakfast became a considerably larger meal, with both hot and cold meats and game being served, in addition to all manner of breads and cakes, plus tea and coffee. It was at this time that the foods the English today associate with a 'proper' breakfast were introduced: sausages, bacon, kippers, haddock, mushrooms and a variety of egg dishes.

Today, because of our hectic lifestyles, people rarely have time to sit down to a proper, leisurely breakfast, so a breakfast party will be all the more enjoyable.

Off the cuff cutlery

While the British and North Americans lay their flatware on the table with the tines of forks and the bowls of spoons facing upwards, the French lay them facing downwards. In the Georgian era, this was also done in Britain, which prevented lacy cuffs from catching on them. Sensibly, the monograms were therefore on the backs of the flatware at this time.

Right (top): *These simple yet elegant silver teaspoons are engraved with the family crest.*

Right (bottom): *China makes an enormous impact on a table setting, even when informally stacked on a buffet table.*

Opposite: *A selection of Georgian and Victorian silver teapots and coffee pots not only are practical but also add richness to this breakfast buffet, complementing the blue-and-white china.*

Farmhouse Tea

Intimate meals, or even just tea with scones and cakes around the kitchen table, can be a delightful way of entertaining friends. Tea and breakfast are my favourite meals. When I have weekend guests to stay in the country, there is nothing I enjoy more than baking a chocolate sponge cake (among my boys' favourites), carrot cake, banana bread or scones for tea. Although it's traditional to serve thick clotted cream and strawberry jam with scones, I prefer them just with butter, which melts into the warm scones. My favourite tea sandwiches are smoked salmon or marmite on brown bread. They should be bite-sized, without crusts and made at the last moment. With home-made cakes, you couldn't have a better welcome for close friends.

The cup runneth over

When tea first became a fashionable drink in the eighteenth century, it was perfectly correct to pour the tea from the cup into the saucer to drink it.

Above: *Tea always tastes better from bone china cups. Here, a gold-and-white tea set, c.1830, has been set out on a large damask cloth with a lacy afternoon tea cloth over the top. Blue-and-white checked tea napkins add a touch of colour.*

Left: *The tea party shown here has been laid out in one corner of a large kitchen in the seventeenth-century farmhouse featured on pages 40–5. The large black range dates from c.1870.*

Opposite: *For a casual tea in a farmhouse kitchen, only the simplest arrangements of garden flowers fit in, such as these branches of blackberries spilling out of a china jug. The other flowers in the room are buddleia and scabious.*

Picnic in Normandy

There is always something wonderfully romantic about a picnic. My fairytale setting for a picnic has water close by and a stunning view, preferably with mountains. The site featured here has the water, but the mountains are replaced by what looks like a fairytale castle. It is, in fact, a Normandy château, the dining room of which is shown on pages 56–61. The château was the home of Diane de Poitiers, mistress of Henri II, in the sixteenth century. In the eighteenth century, the park and gardens were laid out by the famous French landscape architect Le Nôtre, but these were replaced in 1850 with the present landscape, which is less formal and more romantic.

The picnic pictured here has been set out in the shade of a willow tree, next to a canal originally built by Le Nôtre. There are lovely views up to the château and across the water to woods and fields. This is undoubtedly a luxury picnic, which was possible because the food and accessories didn't have to be transported far. Picnics obviously have to be tailored to the location – and also to the people involved, as children's requirements are very different to adults'.

Far more preparation goes into a picnic than many people realize, but the key is to be organized and keep the food simple, with as much as possible of it prepared in advance. Today there are many practical and stylish accessories available for picnics,

Above: *Even when you are surrounded by nature, a simple vase of flowers, such as these cosmos, adds to the sense of occasion.*

Left: *An antique striped picnic rug from India provides a capacious base for this picnic in France.*

Right: *Swans on the canal-side complete the idyllic scene.*

such as Thermos flasks for soup, insulated cool-boxes, unbreakable plastic plates and glasses, lightweight food containers, paper napkins, and picnic rugs with waterproof backings. All of these undoubtedly make eating outdoors safer, more convenient and more comfortable. But if you want to capture some of the romance of the traditional picnic, there is no substitute for old, well-used picnic hampers and baskets, along with real china, glasses and table linen (provided, of course, that you have the strength to carry them!).

Although I personally prefer the simple option of a blanket, there is no doubt that folding chairs and tables can sometimes be useful, so long as you don't have to walk a long way with them. In previous centuries a picnic often entailed being seated in chairs around a trestle table with servants in attendance! For the picnic shown here it was intended that the whole afternoon be spent lazily enjoying the canal-side setting with a few friends. Cards, boules and a backgammon set have been provided for additional entertainment – the only thing missing is a string quartet!

Below left: Antique French table napkins add to the luxury of this picnic.

Below right: Cushions prove very welcome after an hour or so of sitting on the hard ground.

Ground rules

Picnics actually started as informal indoor meals to which everyone contributed a dish, but by the mid-nineteenth century the word had come to mean a meal eaten outdoors. Picnics were the first rule-free meals, and that's probably why they became so popular with the rule-bound Victorians. No cooking, no tables, no chairs – just fresh air, wasps and a general feeling of relief from constraint.

Opposite: Simple finger food that doesn't require any preparation beforehand is best for picnics. Here, a selection of cheeses, salamis, French bread and fresh fruit and vegetables is set out on antique French plates and baskets.

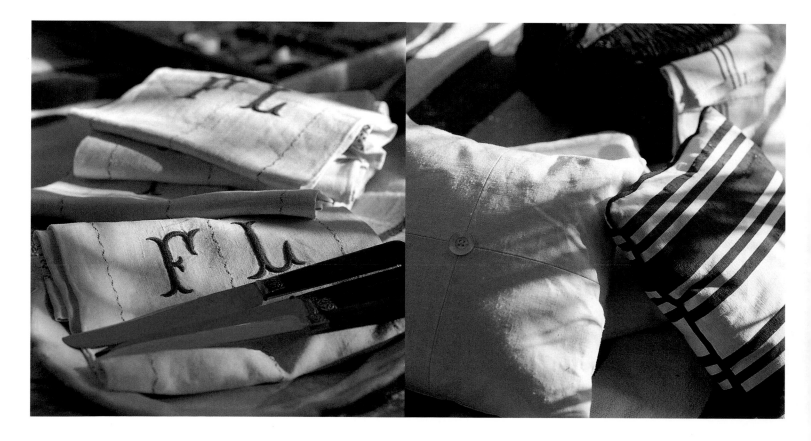

Drinks before Dinner

When guests arrive for dinner, it is important to make them feel relaxed and welcome. Serving drinks is a good way of doing this, particularly as this also gives the cook(s) a chance to complete last-minute preparations in the kitchen. If you serve a variety of light canapés with the drinks, a starter probably won't be necessary at dinner. When you are entertaining a fairly large group, avoid drinks you have to mix, and opt instead for champagne or champagne cocktails, mulled wine or fruit punch. Here, glasses and canapés are set out in the drawing room of a Georgian country house. The double doors of the drawing room lead into the dining room (shown on pages 116–23).

Another way to make guests feel welcome is with flowers and other floral decorations around the house. You can set the scene by decorating the front door with a wreath or garland of seasonal flowers, leaves or berries, and then carry the idea through the entrance hall and into the living room; these flowers will be seen before people even go into dinner. Because guests will not be sitting down around a table at this point, you can indulge yourself with tall, dramatic arrangements that would be too large for a dining table. Branches of leaves or blossom lend themselves well to this and look good with minimal arranging.

Left: *A tantalizing array of hors d'oeuvres, along with glasses for drinks, is set out on a sofa-table in the drawing room. The antique glass-domed 'shade' on the left is of a miniature violin-maker's workshop, which sits permanently on this table.*

Below left: *Ice cubes with tiny fruits frozen in them look much prettier than the plain version. Redcurrants are used here, but small flowers like violets and fragrant sprigs of borage or mint could be used in the same way.*

Below right: *Details such as tinted glassware on an antique engraved silver gallery tray make an evening more special.*

Contact sport

The drinks party is a game of social contact, offering an opportunity to see and be seen rather than the intimacy of a dinner party. People who are 'good' at drinks parties have learned the skills of small talk and how to slide in and out of conversations with charm and ease.

Afternoon Tea

The making and drinking of tea in Britain was once a ritual akin to the Japanese tea ceremony. Because tea was so expensive, it was kept in a locked caddy by the mistress of the house, who made tea for family and friends in the drawing room, using water heated in a silver kettle with a spirit lamp. The precious brewed liquid was then poured into the finest porcelain cups and accompanied by an array of dainty sandwiches, teacakes and larger cakes handed around on exquisite plates. In Victorian times, when this house was built, afternoon tea – which by then was taken between about four o'clock and half-past five – had become a particularly lavish production, offering the ideal opportunity to impress visitors with the hostess's extensive tea service. She would set everything out on a table in the drawing room, and etiquette would be very carefully observed.

Invitations to partake of afternoon tea are perhaps less frequent now, but a well-prepared tea table, or even just a pretty tray of tea things, can be a delight to the eye and the tastebuds. The joy of tea is that it is a portable event. You can take it in the garden if the day is sunny, or indoors when the nights draw in. I prefer it in the relaxed and comfortable ambience of a sitting room, in front of an open fire. And it is still a good opportunity to use and enjoy a fine collection of china cups and saucers. Nevertheless, afternoon tea these days is usually a fairly casual affair. In fact, that is another advantage of a tea: it need not be too formal or follow etiquette too closely.

In this Victorian town house in South-west London, the wall between two rooms was knocked down to form one fairly spacious room that is much more suited to entertaining than the house would have been in Victorian times. The large bay window at each end of the room makes the space much lighter and airier, and, although the window treatments are layered, as in the nineteenth century, the blinds and swags are not at all heavy or oppressive. Similarly, while the architecture and most

Above: *Pink-and-white anemones pick up the colours of this antique vase, creating an arrangement that is as fresh and light as the room itself.*

Left: *A window seat provides an inviting place to enjoy afternoon tea in the drawing room of this nineteenth-century London town house.*

of the furniture and ornaments are Victorian, the use of textiles, the mixture of art and the overall feel of the room are unmistakably contemporary. The result is a room that fits in well with the period of the house and at the same time with the lifestyles and tastes of the occupants.

In such a room, a modern interpetation of the Victorian custom of afternoon tea will not be ostentatious or formal. It includes a charming antique china tea service and embroidered linen, plus home-made cakes with the tea, but everything is set out informally on trays, a chest and an ottoman. This allows the hostess the opportunity to serve her guests. As an alternative, it can be laid out on a table, so that people can help themselves if they wish. And, unlike in Victorian times, hats and gloves are not required for the ladies!

Below left: The drawing room, which is quite long, has been divided into separate sitting areas, making it cosier for the family and more functional when entertaining.

Below right: An ottoman in front of the fire can be used as extra seating, a footrest or a place to put the tea tray.

Opposite, clockwise from top left:
At this informal afternoon tea, guests' teacups and plates can be perched anywhere there is space.

Victoriana is given a strong contemporary twist in this town house.

Part of the pleasure of a proper tea is using beautiful china.

Guests are given tea plates and knives but not forks, so any cakes that are served should not be too crumbly.

Signs of the times

For the last hundred years it has been frowned upon to leave the teaspoon in the teacup rather than on the saucer. Prior to this, however, a spoon standing up in a teacup was a sign that no more tea was wanted. Similarly, to indicate to the hostess that one's cup was empty, either the spoon was laid across the top of the cup or the cup was turned upside-down.

Lunch with a French Accent

Left: *Symmetry and fine architectural detailing play a large part in the elegance of this French dining room.*

Above: *The ceiling depicts symbols associated with Diane de Poitiers and Henri II.*

Below: *The main portal to the Château d'Anet is a triumphal arch built to the glory of Diana, the Roman goddess of the hunt. This is an allusion to Diane de Poitiers, who loved hunting.*

The ritual of dining is always important in France, and whether it is a simple lunch or a formal dinner for twenty people, an equal amount of care and attention is given to the food and decoration. The lunch pictured here takes place at the same location as the dinner featured on pages 56–61, but this dining room is in a separate house in the grounds of the château. The building was originally built for the Château d'Anet's caretaker. As a caretaker was usually a nobleman and perhaps also a relative of the owner, the rooms of a caretaker's house were likely to be of good proportions, with fine architectural features. This house is no exception, and it has wonderful views of the château over the canal, and of parkland.

Because the kitchen in the house is too small to have an eating area, most meals are taken in this dining room. With windows on three sides, the room has the advantage of good natural light all day. So as not to obstruct the light and views, the windows have been left free of curtains and blinds. They do have working shutters, which fold back neatly into the window recesses, but the shutters are generally left

open at night so that the wonderful floodlit views of the château reflected in the canal can be enjoyed.

The panelling, although simple, is supremely elegant, with its limed and aged finish and panels picked out in gilt. One of the most important features of the room is the magnificent Renaissance painted ceiling, decorated with the crescent, fleur-de-lys and intertwined initials of Diane de Poitiers and Henri II (see page 87, top). These motifs are repeated throughout the house, as they are through the château and the grounds.

The dining table is set for an informal Sunday lunch for four, and the setting is deliberately simple to avoid detracting from the spectacular views. Instead of place-mats, plain silver chargers are used as underplates. The wineglasses are similar to those in the château (see pages 59–60), while the blue-and-white china is eighteenth-century and was imported from the East for the Dutch market. The fact that the patterns of the various pieces vary actually makes them more interesting,

Left: *The dining room, though not large, can seat up to ten people when the table is extended. The room benefits from superb views on three sides, so the decoration is monotone to allow the views and architectural features to speak for themselves. Above the oak coffer is a Louis XVI cartel clock.*

Opposite: *The floral arrangement on the carved oak coffer provides the only splash of colour in this dining room, apart from the blue-and-white porcelain. The flowers – roses and Mexican orange blossom – have been picked from the walled cutting garden.*

rather than less. A blue-and-white tureen is used as the centrepiece instead of a flower arrangement, thus keeping the theme to blue and white. The only flowers are placed on the coffer, which functions as a sideboard.

Lunch might consist of a light starter such as soup or a terrine of game or fish, followed by a hot dish of roasted meat and vegetables. No French meal would be complete without a selection of fine wines, carefully chosen to complement the food. Salad served with local cheeses selected from the nearby market would be served before the dessert, as is customary in France, because the French like to eat the cheese with the wine that accompanied the main course. The dessert itself might be a fruit tart or gâteau.

Fine eighteenth-century blue-and-white pots adorn the mantelpiece in the dining room.

Elegant silver chargers are used instead of place-mats underneath the eighteenth-century dinner service.

Soup is a social minefield

In Britain and North America, one 'eats' soup rather than 'drinking' it. British and North American diners sip from the side of the soup spoon, tilting it towards the mouth (to the bemusement of the French and other Europeans, who put the spoon in their mouth). It is the custom to dip the spoon into the soup, pushing the spoon from the front of the bowl to the back until it is about two-thirds full. Because it is not customary to drink wine with this course, soup served at the start of a meal provides a little padding in the stomach before the wine is served. For guests to refuse the soup is churlish, indicating one's hope of filling up with better things. For the host to overfill the soup plates is also very bad form, carrying the message that there's not much to follow.

a sense of
OCCASION

New Year's Eve Buffet

I have always had mixed feelings about New Year's Eve. Coming as it does at the end of the Christmas season, when everyone is tired and overindulged, the last thing we need on the agenda is yet another party. However, once the evening is in full swing and the atmosphere comes alive, everyone ends up having a great time! I think the key is to keep people relaxed and involve all age groups. I prefer to serve a buffet rather than a sit-down dinner, especially if there are a lot of people. Not only is it easier, but it also is more relaxed and gives the guests an opportunity to talk to everyone.

What better way to welcome in the New Year than a buffet dinner in this manor house dating back eight centuries? Set in beautiful parkland and gardens in the Worcestershire countryside, the house is completely surrounded by a wide moat. It was originally built as a medieval 'hall house', within the moat for safety, in the twelfth century. In the Tudor period, a manor house grew up around the hall, which retained its function as the place where meals were taken, and this is the dining room pictured here. The original hammerbeam roof is visible in the photograph opposite. Various changes were made to the house in subsequent centuries, particularly in the mid-nineteenth century with some Gothic-revival additions.

In the Middle Ages, when this hall was built, the entire household, including the family and all the servants, would have eaten together here. Long, narrow trestle tables were set up before each meal. Special banquets were highly theatrical occasions, with a table the equivalent of a stage. The benches were arranged along only one side of each table, so that the crowds of onlookers could observe the spectacle. The lord of the manor, his wife and the most important guests sat at the 'high table' – which was literally higher, as it was usually raised on a dais – at one end of the hall. Women generally sat at separate tables from the men but were not always allowed to attend banquets, so they might watch the proceedings from a gallery or balcony.

Without the food, the tables were unimpressive. Covered with white linen cloths sprinkled with fresh herbs and flowers, they were laid with trenchers (flat, square pieces of bread or wood, used as plates), salt and sometimes large napkins. There might also be spoons, but guests often brought their own, as well as their own knives; forks were not yet in use. A board on trestles – the 'cup-board' or buffet – held an impressive display of drinking vessels in horn, wood, silver or gold. If a person wanted a drink of wine, a cup-bearer was instructed to bring it, and if the drinker was a woman, the cup-bearer might actually hold a napkin under her chin while she drank.

The guests and the food, not the table, were of interest to the onlookers, and the courses were brought in by processions of servants with flaming torches, to the accompaniment of trumpets, drums or bagpipes. At the end of the meal, the bread

A great hall dating back to the twelfth century is the spectacular setting for a New Year's Eve buffet, set out on a large mahogany table.

trenchers, if they hadn't been eaten, and the bones were thrown on the floor for the waiting dogs and cats.

Banqueting had changed considerably by the second half of the nineteenth century, when the Gothic-revival alterations to this room were completed. The guests, in full evening dress, would assemble in the drawing room, where the host would quietly tell each gentleman which lady he was to 'hand in' to dinner. When dinner was announced, the host led the procession into the dining room, with the most important lady on his arm. The remaining guests followed, in order of the woman's rank, finishing with the most important gentleman and the hostess. The host, standing in his place at the bottom of the table, indicated where guests were sitting, as placement cards were not used by high society. The ladies sat to the right of the gentlemen who had escorted them, and the hostess sat at the head of the table.

The table was resplendent with a white damask tablecloth (never place-mats), elaborately folded damask napkins, flowers and fruit, lamps or candelabras, as well as china, crystal and a profusion of silver cutlery – but not food. The dishes were now placed on the sideboard, from which they were handed around to the guests by the butler and footmen, in the new fashion known as service *à la russe*. Women did not ask for wine while seated at the table – their male companions were in charge of serving them. At the end of the meal, the ladies would retire to the drawing room for coffee, leaving the gentlemen to their claret, port and coffee, then the men would join the ladies after only twenty minutes or so.

The nineteenth century also saw the introduction of the 'buffet' meal. At a Victorian buffet meal, the food was laid out on a sideboard or dresser, where everyone would help themselves and then take the food to the table to eat it. Today, buffets are

Below left: A wonderful collection of late nineteenth-century horn-handled flatware and horn-and-silver beakers and jugs looks absolutely at home in this setting.

Below right: Oak panelling and an oil painting form a rich backdrop for a gold candelabra and other gold-plated items on a carved oak side table placed next to the fireplace.

Opposite: I love to see seasonal greenery and a roaring fire at New Year's Eve celebrations, and they set off the dark wood, horn, silver and gold at this party beautifully. The antler candelabras are German, c.1850.

more often laid out not on the sideboard but on the table, as for the buffet dinner pictured here. After serving their plates at the table, the guests at this New Year's Eve celebration will sit on the chairs ranged around the edge of the room and in adjoining rooms to eat. At a buffet, the fact that people won't be seated at the table means that the centrepiece and candles can be taller, making a greater visual statement. The massive holly and fir centrepiece shown here, with the family silver and a collection of horn items, makes a table setting reminiscent of a Scottish New Year's Eve.

New Year celebrations

In Scotland, the celebrations for New Year, known as Hogmanay, overshadow even Christmas, and have not changed for centuries. The focal point of New Year's Eve is the bringing in of a haggis (a large, round sausage made of liver and oatmeal) at just after midnight, as a 'gift to the New Year'. The haggis is traditionally accompanied by a kilted Highlander with bagpipes, and the ceremony includes enthusiastic whisky-drinking.

Right: *I always think that an array of beautiful silverware looks so much nicer than simply rolling up cutlery in a napkin. However, it does take up a lot of room on the table!*

Below: *A Vienna bronze model of a stag, c.1800, nestles into the fir and holly on the dining table.*

Valentine Supper

Valentine's Day, like Christmas, has become so commercialized that the romance and spontaneity are in danger of being lost. If I were planning a Valentine supper at home I would do it in one of two ways. Either it would be incredibly sophisticated, with the best caviare, champagne and fine wine, or it would be completely over-the-top – like the intimate Valentine supper featured here. Simplicity is alien to this look – opulence and extravagance are the keynotes. The drawing room of a late eighteenth-century house in Powys, Wales, is the setting. Ambience is of paramount importance here, and the table lamps, candles and a blazing log fire in the black marble fireplace create a suitably romantic atmosphere for the occasion.

The period of the house is quite appropriate for this meal, because it was during the eighteenth century that intimate suppers for fewer than ten people became popular. The servants would set out the food ahead of time because they would not be present during the meal, and, in at least some instances, romance and seduction were involved. Those suppers would, however, have been held in the dining room.

This house has a large and impressive dining room, as well as a smaller breakfast room (see pages 104–11), but for a *tête-à-tête*, a sumptuously appointed table in a corner of the drawing room is cosier. Two Louis XV *fauteuil* armchairs upholstered in pink tapestry fabric are drawn up to a small, round occasional table for the meal. The Georgian period of the house notwithstanding, a Victorian theme has been used for

Left: *Louis XV armchairs and an antique paisley shawl create a rich backdrop for red and silver table accessories.*

Right: *A modern china coffee cup reinforces the Valentine theme.*

the table setting. Consequently, the table is packed with late Victorian antiques, along with some modern decorative accessories, all matched to the red, pink and silver colour theme.

An antique paisley shawl is used as a tablecloth, and on top of it are placed two beaded place-mats, one red and one silver. The cut-crystal plates and the silver and mother-of-pearl pistol-grip flatware are late Victorian. A candelabra has been borrowed from the mantelpiece. A cranberry-glass wine cooler with a silver rim holds the champagne, and the red wine has been decanted into a ruby cut-glass decanter.

A silver basket is filled with mother-of-pearl hearts in silk purses, silk-ribbon flowers and a large chocolate heart, while an early twentieth-century cigarette box serves as an elegant casket for still more hearts and flowers. Real flowers fill two mother-of-pearl conch shells on the place-mats, while other flowers float in a silver dish. As if all this were not rich enough, a small shell holds some after-dinner chocolate truffles. The overall effect of this Valentine supper setting is completely over-the-top, which was the aim – but just a few of these ideas could be used on their own for a more restrained display.

Right: A heady mixture of warm, rich colours and textures is softened by candlelight at this romantic supper for two.

Below left: Red ranunculus flower-heads floating in a shallow silver dish provide a dramatic centrepiece.

Below right: Each place-setting consists of an antique crystal plate on a beaded place-mat, with a mother-of-pearl conch shell filled with ranunculus and alstroemeria flowers.

A time for lovebirds

Valentines, in the form of cards, love letters and poems, have been exchanged by sweethearts on February 14 ever since the Middle Ages. The day is named after St Valentine, a third-century Roman priest and Christian martyr, who is said to have secretly performed forbidden weddings. However, the date was chosen in the belief that this is the day every year that birds choose their mates.

Easter Brunch

To me Easter always conjures up the arrival of spring – daffodils and tulips, buds on the trees and baby lambs prancing around the greening fields. I like to spend Easter in the country and perhaps have a few friends to stay. Easter Sunday brunch is always a treat to prepare. Although the festival of Easter does not feature much traditional fare, eggs and hot cross buns are always associated with it. One favourite of mine is eggs Benedict, and I also like scrambled eggs with a variety of goodies chopped into them such as black truffles, tomatoes and fresh herbs, or smoked salmon. In addition, I usually serve a whole honey-roast ham, breads, fruit juice and fresh fruit, plus, of course, a choice of coffee or tea. For table decoration I use only spring flowers from the garden. Moss baskets filled with decorated hardboiled eggs are a fun way to involve children, and I like to use table linen and china in springlike yellows, greens and white with a touch of pink.

The table laid here for an Easter brunch is in the breakfast room of a late Georgian house in Powys, Wales (the drawing room of which is featured on pages 100–3). The 'breakfast parlour' and the 'morning room' had been introduced into large country

Above: *Spring flowers abound at this Easter brunch – even the china is covered in flowers.*

Left: *A table setting using fresh pastel colours creates a suitably springlike atmosphere for an Easter brunch in the breakfast room of this late Georgian house.*

houses at about the time this house was built. Sited at the back of the house, with an easterly or south-easterly aspect and large windows, to make the most of the morning light, they reflected the new, less formal approach to family life. Unlike the public rooms of the house, they were designed for use only by the family (or house guests who were close friends), since social visits no longer were taken before noon. Even breakfast parties and the obligatory visits known as 'morning calls' had been moved to the afternoon by the beginning of the nineteenth century.

Initially, breakfast parlours were used for breakfast, and morning rooms only as morning sitting rooms. By the early nineteenth century, however, these functions had generally been combined into a single room known as the morning room, reflecting the fact that it was now acceptable for the family to be present while the servants were clearing the breakfast things away. The room was thus used for late, lingering breakfasts and for idling the morning away reading newspapers and books, playing the piano, writing letters, sewing, playing cards or chatting. Subsequently, in Victorian times, the morning room was used only by the female members of the family, but by the early twentieth century, this custom had been relaxed and the room was once again often enjoyed by the whole family.

The room featured here, with its east-facing windows and its location adjoining the kitchen, is ideal as a breakfast room. In fact, it is also used for family lunches and suppers, as the house's spacious dining room tends to be reserved mainly for large lunch and dinner parties. From the time when breakfast parlours and morning rooms were first introduced, their atmosphere has been light, relaxed and cheerful, with predominantly feminine touches such as gaily decorated china and jardinières of

Below left: Miniature white porcelain urns hold vividly coloured violets.

Below right: This modern china with its egg-and-feather design is well suited to breakfast or brunch, especially at Easter. The napkin has been rolled up and tied with ribbon.

Opposite: Ceramic eggs nestling in moss fill this pretty antique china Easter basket.

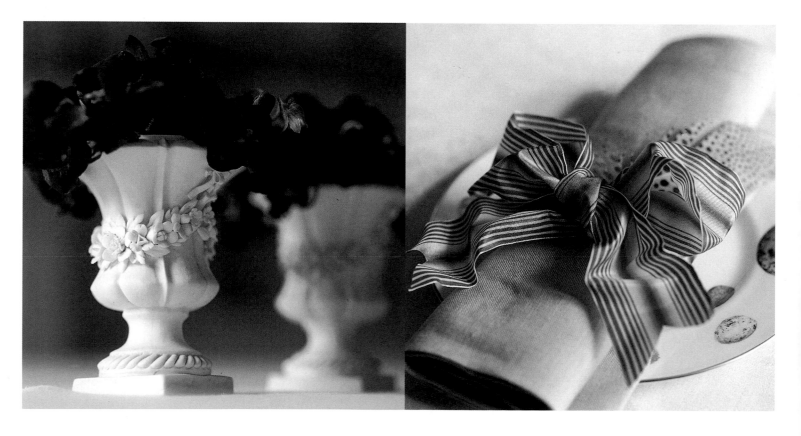

plants and flowers, and this room has been decorated in keeping with that style. The scheme is simple and understated, with the panelled walls, radiators, woodwork, fireplace and mirror frame all painted a muted green, beneath a white ceiling. The chintz curtains and the cotton slipcovers on the dining chairs are in fabrics of the same soft green and white, and the floor covering is wall-to-wall sisal matting. All this forms a perfect background for the collection of china displayed on the walls, on the side table and in the display cabinets which have been built into the alcoves flanking the fireplace.

When this house was built, breakfast china was still a fairly recent development, but by Victorian times a plethora of new pieces had appeared. This was the result of several factors: the evolution of breakfast into a substantial meal in its own right, the rapidly growing popularity of tea and coffee, and the Victorian taste for bric-à-brac and over-refinement.

Breakfast sets could include breakfast cups and saucers (the cups had a capacity of about half a pint/300 millilitres, making them much larger than teacups), breakfast plates (about 1 inch/2.5 centimetres wider than tea plates) and eggcups. Some also included coffee 'cans' (straight-sided cups), a cream jug, milk jug, sugar bowl, teapot and slop bowl (into which the hostess would empty the dregs of tea when refilling a cup – a practice that has generally died out now). The table might also be covered

Opposite: The tassels used to tie up these napkins match the painted egg and marble eggs sitting in a basket of moss.

Below left: Decorating the table with eggs, as well as serving them as part of the meal, celebrates their Easter symbolism.

Below right: A small gift at each place consists of a shell filled with liqueur chocolates and chocolate mini-eggs, wrapped up in cellophane and tied with ribbon and velvet flowers.

with a multitude of extra pieces used for breakfast, such as eggcup stands and baskets, toast racks, bread trays, pots for jam, honey and marmalade, muffin plates with domed covers, roll plates, cake plates, butter dishes, cruet stands and fruit bowls. On the sideboard, there could be a 'nest egg' (a ceramic chicken on a basket, used to keep boiled eggs hot), platters for cold meats, dishes for potted fish, a china drainer for fried food such as bacon or sausages, and covered serving dishes for other hot dishes such as devilled kidneys, mutton cutlets, kedgeree or broiled haddock.

Although today there is not the need – thankfully – for all these items, or for much of the food they contained, they have become highly collectable antiques, which look attractive displayed in a kitchen, breakfast room or dining room. A few selected pieces of decorative china, whether antique or modern, look lovely on a breakfast or brunch table, particularly if some of the items relate to the theme of the occasion, as the egg-patterned china, antique china Easter bonnet and ceramic baskets do here.

Easter customs

The oldest and most important of the Christian festivals, Easter celebrates Christ's resurrection. The name and much of the symbolism, however, are pagan. As Christianity spread, it took over many of the pagan festivals, including the one celebrating the arrival of spring, which was named after Eostre, the Anglo-Saxon goddess of the spring. After a period of fasting, a great feast was held, and gifts of dyed, hard-boiled eggs were exchanged as a symbol of renewed life. There were also egg hunts and egg-rolling contests. Decorated eggs have been associated with Easter ever since. The Easter bunny tradition derives from the ancient symbolism of hares and rabbits to represent new life, and the fact that the hare was sacred to Eostre. At certain festivals, the Saxons, and also the Greeks and Romans, used to eat bread marked with a cross, and this custom, too, was adopted by Christians, in the form of hot cross buns, representing the Crucifixion.

Opposite: *More china and flowers decorate a side table, where a blue-and-white china dish is filled with primulas, narcissi, hyacinths and muscari, and a glass vase holds amaryllis.*

Top right: *Narcissi and muscari look charming encircling the rim of this antique china Easter bonnet.*

Centre right: *Lemon cakes hollowed out and filled with chocolate mini-eggs are arranged on a ceramic basket.*

Bottom right: *An antique jug holds colourful narcissi and muscari. Placing small arrangements of different combinations of the same flowers around the room helps to reinforce the theme and tie all the elements together.*

Halloween Buffet

Generally a time for children, Halloween actually provides a great theme for an adult party, with atmospheric decorations based on candlelight. The Halloween buffet pictured here is set in a modern conservatory in a London town house. The fact that a conservatory is an outdoor room makes it seem as though the party is being held outside, while everyone is actually benefiting from the comfort and warmth of the house. In the surrounding darkness the flickering light and deep shadows cast by a multitude of jack-o'-lanterns and other candles create a magical effect that puts everyone in the right mood.

Although the designs cut into these jack-o'-lanterns are hardly fierce enough to frighten away evil spirits, they still create a beautiful warm glow. They are most effective when used *en masse*, in this case grouped together on a Victorian wirework plant stand. Candelabras, multi-wick candles, night-lights (votives) and hurricane lamps have all been used, in addition to beeswax candles stuck in terracotta pots filled with sand or marbles. As a result, any additional lighting, which in this case would detract from the dramatic atmosphere, is unnecessary.

Because the conservatory is too small for a sit-down meal, a buffet is the obvious answer for entertaining a group of people, even though at the end of October they are unlikely to be able to spill out onto the lawn. A buffet also has the advantage of freeing the hostess, since there is no first course to serve, and the main course and dessert can be set out in advance. Furthermore, there is no seating plan to worry about, because guests sit or stand wherever they like; and an extra guest – or a cancellation – doesn't create a problem.

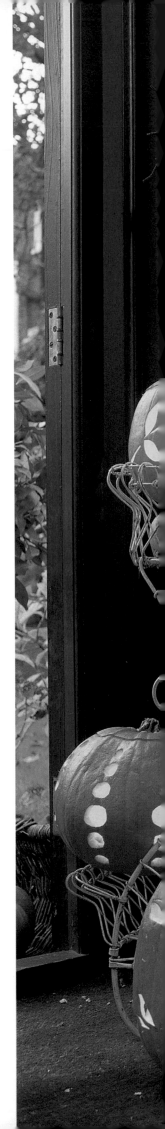

Left: *Hanging from a length of twine strung over a sofa in the conservatory are night-lights (votives) in glass jars and in home-made paper lanterns (which should never be left unattended once lit), strings of Chinese lanterns and bundles of cinnamon sticks tied with raffia.*

Right: *Jack-o'-lanterns on a wirework stand, a dried eucalyptus leaf wreath and a twig tree decorated with quinces and crab apples are among the decorations for this Halloween party.*

The food, plates and flatware can be set out on one or more tables, either against a wall, as here, or away from the wall so that guests can approach both long sides at once, which speeds up the serving process. Here, to maintain the dark background, a small, chocolate-coloured linen tablecloth is laid over a beige check linen cloth covering the table. The napkins match the darker cloth, and the plates are beige with a brown rim. The serving dishes, ranging from stone platters to gnarled wood dishes, look like they have come straight out of an enchanted forest.

Halloween offers an irresistible opportunity to indulge oneself with colourful decorations associated with the season. Here, gourds, Chinese lanterns, apples, quinces and crab apples, cinnamon sticks, nuts, figs, autumn leaves, and a wreath of dried eucalyptus leaves provide splashes of colour in the candlelight.

Left: *Limestone and gnarled wood platters and dishes accentuate the organic quality of the buffet table.*

Below left: *Ripe figs are set off to perfection by the light from an iron candelabra.*

Below right: *Large, red-tinged leaves clipped with an old-fashioned wooden clothes-peg make a striking napkin holder.*

High spirits

All Hallows' Eve, or Halloween – when the dead were said to return to earth in the form of ghosts, witches and goblins, and the powers of darkness took over from the sun – used to be marked by dancing around huge bonfires and praying for the souls in purgatory while holding flaming torches aloft. Everyone then returned home to feast on roasted apples, seedcake and spiced ale, tell ghost stories around the fire in the grate, and try to foretell the future using apples, nuts and candles. The favourite game, then as now, was bobbing for apples (trying to bite apples floating in water). Fierce, glowing jack-o'-lanterns were used to frighten away the evil spirits from the home.

A Family Thanksgiving

Thanksgiving dinner – or, indeed, any harvest supper – provides a splendid opportunity to celebrate autumn's rich abundance and beauty. Family members come from far and wide to gather around a table that is a feast of colours, textures and tastes.

This is such a well-loved family occasion in North America that no one would want to omit any of the traditional elements, but within that framework it is possible to be as lavish and inventive as you like in the menu and table decorations. Harvest suppers are basically very similar – after all, Thanksgiving began as a harvest festival. The first one was in 1621, when the Pilgrim colony at Plymouth, Massachusetts, proclaimed a day of thanksgiving for their first successful harvest. Their native friends were invited to the celebrations and contributed wild turkeys to the feast. Turkey is still traditionally served today, along with cranberry sauce, stuffing, sweet potatoes, mashed potatoes and gravy, followed by pumpkin pie. This holiday – which now falls on the fourth Thursday of November in the United States and on the second Monday of October in Canada – is the most important family celebration of the year.

At such special occasions, creating the right atmosphere is paramount. Fortunately, nature makes it easy at this time of year. The thought of Thanksgiving and harvest suppers immediately conjures up the rich, warm colours and abundant produce of autumn, which are always the keynotes of the celebration. The table decoration can be as sumptuous as the one pictured here, or it can be a simple centrepiece – but it

Left: *A table decoration for Thanksgiving dinner or a harvest supper ought to reflect the rich colours and abundant harvest of autumn.*

Right: *In this eighteenth-century house, a pair of blackamores frames the double doors connecting the drawing room and dining room and draws guests' eyes towards the table laid for dinner.*

Left: *Even the food matches the colour scheme here! A hollowed-out pumpkin holds caramelized orange segments dipped in chocolate.*

would be sacrilege not to make the most of the season's flaming reds and golds, mellow plums and russets, and burnished browns. Most autumn produce is in this colour range, be it leaves, flowers, seedheads, nuts, gourds or fruit, which means you will have a vast selection of material to choose from.

On the table shown here, a large central arrangement in a wire basket holds a candle plus a variety of plant material, including leaves, seedheads, Chinese lanterns, bundles of cinnamon-sticks and dried orange slices. Each of the two smaller arrangements flanking it also holds a candle, along with leaves, ornamental peppers and tangerines.

Clustered around the central arrangement and linking it to the other two are masses of fruit, gourds, small pumpkins, ornamental peppers and dried corncobs. Interspersed among them are foam balls covered with dried material or string, adding even more textural interest to the display. Between the arrangements are antique wire obelisks and antique candlesticks depicting Egyptian, Roman and African figures.

Left: *White linen napkins embroidered with the family's initials and tied with cranberry-coloured ribbon would make an attractive alternative to the sky-blue napkins used for our table setting.*

Right: *The centrepiece extends for virtually the full length of the table, and incorporates no less than nine candles.*

Below: The soft glow of the candles in the chandelier is reflected in the mirror over the fireplace. The plum and blue tribal cotton tablecloth makes a good backdrop for the autumnal decoration – and for the vivid blue china and lighter blue goblets and napkins.

Striking as this table decoration is, there are some practical considerations to keep in mind. In the first place, when arrangements take up this much table space, the serving dishes of food have to be placed between the diners or on a nearby sideboard. If your table is smaller than this one (which seats ten comfortably), the decoration needs to be scaled down accordingly. Also, remember not to make the centrepiece so high that it blocks sight lines. Of course, if particular family members do not get along well, such a barrier could be a distinct advantage!

There are two things that I particularly love to see on this sort of occasion: a roaring log fire and candlelight, both of which help to create an inviting ambience. The chandelier in this room holds candles, supplementing the nine candles on the

Opposite: Each blue napkin is adorned with love-in-a-mist seedheads, Chinese lanterns and orange ribbon, and sits on a Spode Copeland plate.

table and creating a wonderful atmosphere. Remember that the flame of a candle should be well clear of the rest of the table centrepiece and should not be left unattended, as dry leaves, seedheads and similar material are highly inflammable.

An open fire looks glorious in a dining room, but think about comfort too. A fire is not a good idea if anyone will have to be seated close to the fireplace. A large dining room is necessary if hot-back syndrome is to be avoided! Here, as with all entertaining, if you keep the comfort and pleasure of your guests at the top of your list of priorities, your occasion is likely to be a success.

Doing the honours

The ceremony of carving meat, game and poultry at the table has been of great importance for centuries. In the Middle Ages the person 'doing the honours', as carving was called, might be a son, other relative or friend of the lord of the manor, and because of the association with knives, as well as the skill involved in the procedure, he was accorded great respect. Carving was seen as an essential part of a nobleman's education, and 'doing the honours' skilfully was a sign of good breeding.

Left: *Additional seating, away from the dining table, adds another dimension to a dining room. In this home, views of the garden can be enjoyed from the window seats, which are not obstructed by curtains.*

Right: *The autumnal theme can be carried through to the decorations elsewhere in the dining room. Here, sitting on a round pedestal table, is a simple wire basket filled with Chinese lanterns, pears, gourds and pine cones, echoing not only the dining table centrepiece, but also the wall colour and the tapestry behind the table, and providing a link between all these elements.*

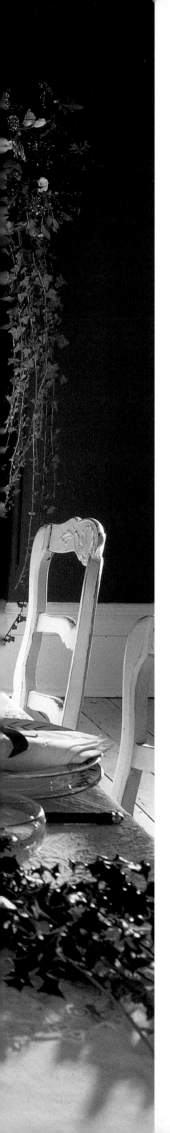

Christmas Lunch

What I really love about Christmas are the traditions behind it, especially decorating the house and sharing Christmas lunch with family and friends. I used to stick to traditional red, green and gold decorations but a few years ago changed to blue, silver and gold coupled with lots of glass balls and white lights for the tree.

I haven't cooked many Christmas lunches, but when I do, I prepare as much as possible in advance so that Christmas morning can be spent opening stockings in bed, attending church and going for a brisk walk to work up an appetite. Although a starter is not really necessary for Christmas lunch, I do still like to serve a light fish dish such as smoked salmon or a shellfish salad. With the turkey I serve all the trimmings – sausages wrapped in bacon, roasted chestnuts, freshly made bread sauce with cloves, rich gravy and cranberry sauce, as well as roast potatoes, brussels sprouts and puréed carrots. We usually finish with Christmas pudding made by an old Austrian cook of my mother's.

A sumptuous table laid for Christmas lunch always looks wonderful, but how many of us have the time at Christmas to gild pine cones and wire apples and nuts? The beauty of the table featured here is that it looks festive and welcoming but will not require enormous amounts of time or skill. Because this Christmas lunch will be shared by family and perhaps a couple of close friends, the setting deliberately avoids being too grand or formal.

Left: *The red walls of this Victorian dining room create an appropriate background for a festive table. A miniature orange tree surrounded by Christmas decorations and greenery forms a dramatic centrepiece.*

Right: *A side table decorated with holly, ivy and pomanders holds a mixture of antique and modern serving pieces. The cut-glass candelabra and the cut-glass claret jug with silver lid are both Victorian, as is the china vegetable dish, while the silver-plated bowl and the flatware are contemporary.*

The house picured here dates from the Victorian era, when many of the traditions we associate with Christmas were introduced. The custom of giving gifts on Christmas Eve or Christmas Day was also begun by the Victorians – previously, gifts had been exchanged on St Nicolas's Day (December 6) or at New Year, but not to the same extent. Many other Christmas customs derived from pagan traditions, including drinking hot mulled wine, eating Christmas cake and pudding, hanging mistletoe above the threshold, decking the house with holly and ivy, and decorating trees.

The dining room walls of this house in West London are painted a deep raspberry-red, which became the keynote for the table decoration. Because the beautiful antique embroidered tablecloth that was to be used on the table was actually too small for it, a plain white damask cloth was used to cover the table first and then the antique cloth was laid over the top. Antique embroidered napkins were used, too, although they are not actually part of a set with the tablecloth.

I like unmatched sets of linen, china and glassware, so long as the pieces look right together. At any rate, when antiques are used, mixing them is often unavoidable. Here, the two antique wineglasses and the reproduction Georgian water tumbler used at each place don't match at all, but they look lovely together, as they are delicate and old-fashioned. (The engraved goblets are late nineteenth-century French, and the pressed-glass goblets are 1920s English.) The antique china is also a mixture – some

Opposite top and opposite bottom right: Victorian-style painted-metal toys make charming table or tree decorations, reminiscent of an old-fashioned Christmas.

Opposite far left: Pomanders piled up in a silver bowl add the scent of Christmas to a room.

Right top: Each of the embroidered napkins is folded into a triangle and tied with a red velvet ribbon decorated with a large ivy leaf. The napkins, china, wine goblets and finger-bowls are all Victorian.

Right bottom: An embroidered antique tablecloth provides an exquisite background not only for tableware but also for baubles and hand-made tree decorations.

pieces have a cobalt blue and gilt wheatsheaf border, while others have a cobalt blue rim with gold dots. Because the colours match, the mix looks good – some would say more interesting than a perfectly matched set!

With these antique table linens, glassware and china, the obvious flatware to choose would be silver in a traditional design – but instead, modern cutlery with round handles that are the exact colour of the walls has been used. The same colour is picked up in the velvet ribbon tied around each white napkin along with a large, deep green ivy leaf which complements the ribbon perfectly. This treatment, in which the napkins are loosely folded into triangles, couldn't be simpler and takes only a few minutes to do, yet it looks very festive.

Left: *Coloured baubles hang from twisted willow branches, framing the Victorian mirror over the mantelpiece.*

Below: *The mantelpiece greenery is complemented by red decorations, including candle-lanterns, hand-made tree decorations and faux berries.*

The table centrepiece is equally quick to assemble, because it is based upon a miniature orange tree growing in a pot. Fir is arranged around the pot and, with holly, extends out to the corners of the table. As well as the small orange fruits and the red holly berries, splashes of colour come from tree decorations, mercury-glass grapes and a few red velvet roses scattered among the greenery. Also on the table are a pair of mid-nineteenth-century opaline lustre candelabra and several late Victorian salt cellars. (The enormous silvered-glass balls clustered around the base of the centrepiece are Victorian 'witch's balls'. Originally hung in the entrance halls or windows of houses to ward off the evil eye, witch's balls were subsequently hung on Christmas trees and are thought to have been the origin of the smaller baubles in use today.) Although most of the items on the table are antique, a very similar effect would be possible using modern pieces.

The decorations around the dining room are also straightforward. At one end of the room are two nineteenth-century limestone columns from Malta, and on top of each is a container filled with floral foam which holds laurustinus, holly, white lisianthus, trailing ivy and red velvet roses.

The decoration of mantelpieces is always important at Christmas, whether the fireplace is in a sitting room or in a dining room. Here, fir boughs fill the mantelpiece and are brightened with faux holly berries, red velvet roses, hand-made baubles and red candle-lanterns. Branches of twisted willow (which have been stuck in floral foam hidden in the fir) are secured at either side of the large mirror over the fireplace. From these branches hang small tree decorations.

Raising Your Glasses

A 'toast' is so called after the old English custom of floating a piece of toast in the loving cup, which was passed around from guest to guest, brimming with wine, mead or ale. When it reached the host, he was expected to drink the bowl dry and consume the toast in honour of the guests. At one stage, toasting got quite out of hand, becoming little more than a drinking game, and by the late nineteenth century, constant toasting was regarded as rather vulgar. Today, it is done on special occasions such as Christmas and wedding celebrations, and everyone has a glass to themselves. After the toast has been proposed, the glasses are raised and sometimes also 'clinked', everyone looks at the person being toasted (if present) then the wine or champagne is sipped. Etiquette dictates that the host always be given the first chance to propose the toast, and that a guest must ask the host's permission to give a toast.

Coloured baubles, greenery and candlelight unify the table and mantelpiece decorations, while the colour of the cutlery handles, of the ribbons tied around the napkins and the red velvet roses echoes that of the dining room walls.

DIRECTORY

China

The element on the dining table that creates the biggest impact is usually the china. Traditionally, one set is used for everyday meals and casual entertaining, and a second set for special occasions. Although entertaining has become increasingly relaxed, this is still a good system if you wish to entertain with more formal dinner parties or make holiday meals, such as Christmas, special.

The everyday set is generally pottery – either earthenware or stoneware – while the special-occasion set is usually bone china or possibly porcelain. Earthenware, despite being heavy and robust-looking, is the weakest type of ceramic and chips easily; however, it is colourful and cheerful, and usually relatively inexpensive. Examples of some lovely Scandinavian earthenware are shown on pages 135 (bottom left) and 137 (top left). Stoneware, which is stronger and thicker than earthenware, is very durable. Bone china contains bone ash to make it white and translucent; though delicate, it is surprisingly strong. Porcelain is fine, translucent and very delicate and is deservedly referred to as the 'queen of ceramics'. Glass plates and dishes can also look lovely – see page 148 (bottom right).

Although antique porcelain and bone china is undeniably beautiful, it is possible to achieve a very similar effect with contemporary china. A few eighteenth-century and many nineteenth-century patterns are still being manufactured today by such companies as Wedgwood, Crown Derby, Royal Worcester, Spode and Limoges, and there are also innumerable contemporary patterns that are as classic as any antiques. All of the pieces illustrated in this Directory are contemporary; the sources are listed on page 160.

According to traditional etiquette, the china for a formal dinner party should all be from the same set, although the dessert china can be different if wished. However, it is fashionable now to mix china, so you may wish to relax the rules – though for it to look right, the pieces do need to be linked in some way. Different patterns in the same colour, or combination of colours, can look good together, as can the same pattern in different colours, such as the set shown on page 137 (bottom right). For both earthenware and stoneware, mixing is even more prevalent now.

Plain white china is the most versatile, or you could choose the classic combination of white with a coloured border and a gold rim. A cobalt-coloured rim is particularly traditional. China with a simple

pattern is also quite adaptable, while an elaborate pattern makes more of a visual statement. If you love the pattern, that's fine, but bear in mind that patterned china gives you less scope for varying the other elements of the table setting.

Most dinner services are sold as basic five-piece place-settings, consisting of a dinner plate, dessert or salad plate, bread plate, cup and saucer. You may also wish to buy soup plates or bowls, cereal bowls, underplates and serving pieces such as sauceboats, platters, vegetable dishes and a soup tureen. In addition, you could get a coffee set, consisting of a coffee pot, creamer, sugar bowl and demi-tasse cups and saucers. You will need at least eight place-settings for your dinner service, but ten or twelve is preferable, because this gives you a little leeway in case a piece is chipped or broken and it also allows you to entertain larger parties in style.

A tea set consists of a teapot, milk jug and sugar bowl, plus teacups and saucers and possibly side plates; a cake stand and sandwich tray could be bought individually. A tea set known as a *tête-à-tête* set, such as the one pictured on this page (top right), serves just two people.

If the tea, coffee and dinner services are all in the same pattern, some of the pieces can be used interchangeably.

Glassware

Glassware quite literally makes your table setting sparkle. The variety of contemporary designs is extraordinary, as you can choose from many different shapes, styles, colours and methods of decoration. As the rest of this book demonstrates, there are some exquisite antique pieces, but modern glassware is beautiful, too – and much more affordable. Some of today's manufacturers, such as Waterford, Thomas Webb & Son, Baccarat and St Louis, are still reproducing designs they produced in the eighteenth and nineteenth centuries, and there are also many exciting contemporary designs that fit in well with traditional table settings. All the glassware pictured in this Directory is contemporary – see page 160 for the sources.

As with china, many people prefer to save their best wineglasses for more formal occasions and use an everyday set at other times, particularly as the finest pieces are not necessarily dishwasher-proof. Crystal, the best glass, contains lead, which lends brilliance and clarity as well as weight. 'Lead crystal' contains 24 per cent lead, while 'full lead crystal', the most expensive, contains 30 per cent lead. Full lead crystal is often hand-blown. Some glassware is left completely free of embellishment, while other designs are decorated in various ways, such as engraving, gilding, painting with enamel paints or cutting into facets. A piece of hand-blown, hand-cut, full lead crystal is, in effect, an individual work of art.

Coloured glass has always been popular and has recently become particularly fashionable. Many of the designs of glasses available today, whether traditional reproductions or innovative modern designs, are truly irresistible, ranging from a hint of colour through deep, rich shades to multi-coloured effects. Among the most charming are the relatively inexpensive Moroccan mint-tea glasses, such as those shown on page 32 (top).

Wine connoisseurs prefer to use glasses made from clear glass, so that the colour of the wine can be appreciated. It may, therefore, be better to restrict the use of coloured glasses to pre-dinner drinks or water. The best all-purpose shape for appreciating the bouquet of the wine is the tulip or bowl shape, which tapers towards the rim. A glass that holds 140ml (7 fluid ounces) when filled to the top is the ideal size – however, it should be only half (or, at the most, two-thirds) filled so that the wine can be swirled around and the bouquet fully appreciated.

Although red and white wine can be served from the same shape of glass, the glasses traditionally associated with them reflect the ways they are held. Because a glass of white wine, which is served chilled, is held by the stem so as to avoid warming it up with the hand, these glasses have taller stems. A glass of red wine, which is usually served at room temperature, is sometimes cradled in the hand, so glasses for red wine are also rounder and slightly larger. Water goblets look like large wineglasses, though short, straight-sided tumblers may be used instead. Champagne glasses should be tall, slim 'flutes', which preserve the bubbles longer than the wide, shallow type. Sherry and port glasses are small, narrow versions of wineglasses, and liqueur glasses are smaller still. Brandy balloons (snifters), with their broad, very tapering bowls, should not be so large as to be difficult to cradle in the hand.

At the table, when a water goblet and glasses for white and red wines are used, they are put together at each place setting above the knives; there are no hard-and-fast rules governing their arrangement. Port, brandy or liqueur glasses can be brought in at the end of the meal. As with china, there is no reason that glasses from different sets cannot be mixed, though they will probably look better if there is something, such as colour or style, to link them.

Before the meal or at drinks parties, serve neat spirits in short tumblers, and long mixed drinks in tall tumblers, also known as highball glasses. For drinks parties, at which people tend to forget where they have put their drinks down, allow twice as many glasses as there are guests.

There are many other glass items that can be used on the table, including small salt cellars and butter dishes, compotiers (large, footed bowls), tazze (footed saucers), trifle dishes and other serving dishes, coasters, finger-bowls, candlesticks, vases, underplates and even the dinner plates themselves (such as the one shown on page 148, bottom right).

Decanters and jugs can be used for red wine, port and spirits and look splendid on either the table or the sideboard. Gilded and engraved glass was more typical of eighteenth-century decanters, while cut glass became popular in the nineteenth century. The Victorian claret jug, often with a silver collar, hinged lid, and glass or silver handle (as pictured on page 125), is another popular design still available today. Water jugs, too, come in lovely designs, and these days even mineral water is available in pretty frosted-glass bottles that won't detract from the table setting.

Flatware

It's not necessary to have inherited the family silver – modern silverware will also enhance the table, as the examples on this page and opposite prove. (For sources see page 160.) Many traditional patterns are still manufactured today, including King's (this page, below right), Dubarry, Bead, Rattail, La Régence and Old English. Alternatively, sleek, modern designs, like the flatware pictured opposite, have a sculptural quality and classic simplicity. Silverware is either solid (sterling) silver or silverplate, but the handles are often of other materials – traditionally bone, horn or wood, and these days acrylic resin. Other treatments include enamelling and gold plating (this page, bottom left). It is a good idea to have a set of everyday, stainless steel cutlery that can be put in the dishwasher, and save the silver for special occasions.

Essential pieces of flatware are dinner knives and forks, bread knives, salad or dessert forks, dessert spoons, soup spoons, teaspoons and serving spoons. You might also want fruit knives and forks (since at formal dinners fruit is not eaten with the fingers), fish knives and forks, grape scissors, salad servers and a cake slice.

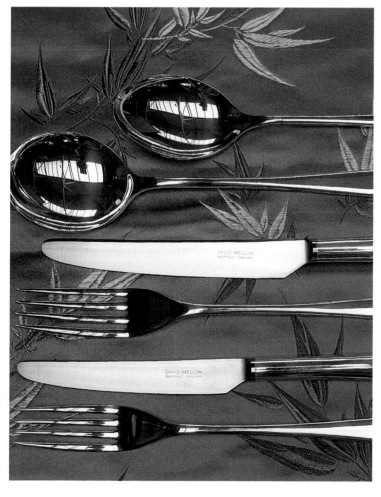

Table Linen

Whether cheerful checks, beautiful cutwork or formal damask, the linen sets the tone for a table. It will complement the tableware to perfection, adding softness to the otherwise hard elements of tabletop, china, glassware and cutlery.

Formal dinners are traditionally set with crisp white damask, with its discreet woven-in white pattern. Traditionally made from linen, but now more often from cotton, damask should ideally be starched and ironed on the wrong side to protect its sheen.

There are many alternatives to damask, including plain linen either unembellished or decorated with a drawn threadwork or other embroidered border, a band in a contrasting colour, braid or lace trim or a self-fringe. Cotton embroidered with cutwork, cross-stitch, monograms or machine embroidery looks lovely, too. Easy-care blends of cotton and polyester demand less ironing.

Antique table linen is still widely available, but contemporary versions can also look extremely attractive – and stains become less of a worry! All of the photographs on pages 148–51 show contemporary examples; for the sources see page 160.

An openwork or lace cloth allows the table surface to show through. Alternatively, it can be laid over an undercloth, either white like the top cloth for a white-on-white effect, or in a contrasting colour. Place-mats allow even more of the table to show or can be used on top of a tablecloth in a contrasting colour. Simple white linen place-mats, as pictured on page 148 (bottom right), look very pretty, while damask table mats on top of a damask cloth in a different colour create an elegant look (as on page 60). Placed along the centre of the tablecloth, a coloured runner is another way of adding contrast. If you prefer a more dramatic look, richly patterned fabric like paisley or a tribal cotton (such as the tablecloth shown on page 120) makes a beautiful background for tableware. For informal entertaining, coloured linen or checked cotton looks fresh and appealing.

Napkins – which can either match or contrast – can be folded or they can be rolled up in a napkin ring. Rings come in a variety of materials, including pewter, china, wood and tortoiseshell. Alternatively, something can be tied around the rolled-up napkin, for example a circlet of ivy or a ribbon, perhaps combined with flowers, leaves, berries or seedheads. Party favours, such as cellophane-wrapped petits-fours or tiny sachets of pot-pourri, could even be tucked inside.

Place Cards

Like improvised napkin rings, place cards provide an opportunity to create a colourful and personal flourish at each place-setting, and they are very useful when there are a lot of dinner guests. Pretty and sometimes amusing place-card holders are available in materials like silver, pewter and china, such as the ceramic flower card-holder opposite (top left). They can also be improvised, as demonstrated by the other examples on these two pages (see page 160 for sources). Table accessories like salt cellars, salt and pepper shakers and miniature candlesticks (such as the one shown on page 16) can all double as place-card holders.

Another idea is to combine each place card with a party favour, such as a hand-made Christmas tree decoration (opposite page, bottom left, and this page, bottom left), a basket of sugared chocolate 'pebbles' (opposite page, top right) or pretty sugar grapes (this page, top right).

The place card itself can be written in an attractive hand, such as a calligraphy script, on stiff card or perhaps hand-made paper. On formal occasions, the full name including the title (Miss, Dr, etc) should be given, but at other times the first name is enough.

Flowers

Flowers for the table need not be elaborate or grand. Often the simplest arrangements are the most memorable, particularly if they incorporate flowers picked from the garden. A centrepiece needs to look good from all sides and relate in shape and size to the table itself, but it should not be so wide that there is no room for food or so tall that it obscures sight lines. Arrangements below eye level are the most usual, but tall arrangements add another dimension. To prevent them from getting in the way visually, choose long-stemmed flowers that will be above eye level. Alternatively, place a tall arrangement at each end of a long table and then seat guests only at the sides; or put it at one side of a square table, and use the other three sides for seating. (Flowers for buffet tables can, of course, be taller.) Instead of a centrepiece, a small bunch of flowers can be put at each lady's place, or a single flower-head can be floated in a finger-bowl for each guest.

Shown on this page are (top) peonies, euphorbia (*E. marginalis* and *E. polychroma*), and ivy berries; and (bottom) hyacinths. Pictured opposite are (clockwise from top left) ranunculus; chincherinchees and pittosporum; roses and euphorbia; and hyacinths.

Candles

Candlelight is unsurpassed for creating a magical atmosphere, and candles are also valuable for adding height to an otherwise flat table-scape. Today a huge range of holders is available, ranging from glass or silver candlesticks (see this page, bottom left and bottom right) to splendid candelabra. There are candle sconces to mount on the walls and huge wood or iron church candlesticks to sit on the floor. Candles now come in an enormous choice of shapes, including fat, multi-wicked, scented candles and candles in glass goblets (see opposite, top right), as well as night-lights (votives) and novelty shapes like fruit and flowers. Often candles don't need holders and can perhaps be combined with plant material, such as cone-shaped candles with pine cones (opposite, bottom right) or a fat beeswax candle with ornamental cabbages (opposite, top left). Floating candles look wonderful with flower-heads in a glass dish (opposite, bottom left) or finger-bowls, while candle shades (this page, top right) create a special sense of occasion. Never to leave burning candles unattended, particularly if you are using candle shades or floral material with them. For the sources of the candles shown here, see page 160.

Index

Acknowledgements

The author would like to thank clients, friends and acquaintances who so kindly agreed to their properties being featured and for their generous cooperation. The sense of style would not be complete without two very capable people, Andreas von Einsiedel, the photographer, and Rose Hammick, the stylist, and I am most grateful to them for their professionalism, wonderful contacts and, most importantly, sense of humour! The team at Collins & Brown has produced another masterpiece, and my particular thanks go to Kate Kirby, Christine Wood and my editor, Alison Wormleighton. Lastly, but by no means least, special thanks to Maggie Pearlstine, my nothing-less-than-erudite agent.

The publishers would like to thank the following for their kind cooperation: HRW Antiques, 26 Sulivan Rd, London SW6 3DX; Annabel Elliot at Talisman Antiques, Gillingham, Dorset; Penny Morrison of Morrison Interiors, 91 Jermyn St, London SW1Y 6JB; Caroline Paterson of Paterson Gornall Interiors, 50 Lavender Gardens, London SW11 1DN; Claire Farrow; Vicky Robinson; and Carol Hammick and Adam Tindle.

In addition, the publishers would like to thank the following, who loaned props for the photographs:

pp12–17: Napkins, silver baskets, serving-spoon warmer – *Guinevere*, 574–580 Kings Rd, London SW6 2DY. Epergne, silver candleholder and baby candle – *The Dining Room Shop*, 62–64 White Hart Ln, London SE13 OPZ. Miniature silver baskets, coffee cups and saucers – *The General Trading Company*, 144 Sloane St, London SW1X 9BL. Glass urns, tazza and salt cellar – *William Yeoward*, 336 Kings Rd, London SW3 5UR. Cheese knife – *Ever Trading*, 12 Martindale, London SW14 7AL. Chocolates – *Rococo*, 321 Kings Rd, London SW3 5EP.

pp18–23: Silver shell place-card holders – *The Dining Room Shop*, as above. Silver roses – *Rococo*, as above.

pp24–7: Ivory-handled knives – *Guinevere*, as above. Knife rests – *Ever Trading*, as above.

pp28–33: Muslin tablecloth and runner – *The Conran Shop*, Michelin House, 81 Fulham Rd, London SW3 6RD. Mirror napkins, tea glasses, mother-of-pearl spoons and salt-and-pepper pots, linen place-mat (p32) – *Maryse Boxer* at Joseph, 26 Sloane St, London SW1X 7LQ. Cutlery – *Ever Trading*, as above. Glass plates, gold napkins (used as place-mats), red vase, candelabra – *Guinevere*, as above. 'Fontainebleau' hock glasses (pp28, 30), 'Tommy' glasses (p29), 'Thistle' hock glasses and flutes (p31),

'Bubbles' hock glass (p32, bottom), coasters – *Thomas Goode & Co*, 19 South Audley St, London W1Y 6BN. Amethyst goblet (p32, bottom) – *William Yeoward*, as above. Epergne, flutes, jug (p33) – *The Dining Room Shop*, as above.

pp40–5: Minton dinner service, gold-rimmed finger-bowls, napkins, pair of painted comports and pink finger-bowl (p44) – *The Dining Room Shop*, as above. 'Leonora' tumblers and goblets, blue goblets (p43) – *William Yeoward*, as above. Enamelled coffee spoons – *Thomas Goode & Co*, as above. Bristol green decanters and goblets (p40) – *Guinevere*, as above.

pp46–51: Contemporary pewter candlesticks, dish, plates, lidded pot (all on dining table), flat-backed candle-holders (p46, far left), glass decanters (p47, far right), napkin rings (p51) – *Ever Trading*, as above. Antique pewter candlesticks (on side table in alcove, p46) – *The Dining Room Shop*, as above. Goblets (p49) – *Guinevere*, as above.

pp52–5: Antique French tablecloth and napkins – *Guinevere*, as above. Bath china – *The Conran Shop*, as above.

pp64–5: 'Alice' china by Gien, cutlery – *The General Trading Company*, as above. Antique white lace napkins – *Braemar Antiques*, 113 Northcote Rd, London SW11 6PW. Glassware – *William Yeoward*, as above. Ceramic sleigh vases, white glass nest-egg, antique miniature mugs used as egg-cups – *The Dining Room Shop*, as above.

pp66–9: Tent – *The Raj Tent Club*, 36a Lansdowne Crescent, London W11 2NT (mail-order available). Rug – *Sinclair Till*, 793 Wandsworth Rd, London SW8 3JQ. Cashmere throw, 'Renaissance' decanter – *The General Trading Company*, as above. Organza tablecloth – *Dickens & Jones*, 224–244 Regent St, London W1A 1DB. Glass urn – *William Yeoward*, as above. Etched-glass plates and goblets and pewter underplates – *Ever Trading*, as above. Antique glass tazza (p68), agate-handled gold flatware (p69), Edwardian tablecloth and Moser flutes (both p67) – *Guinevere*, as above.

pp70–3: Breads, cakes, etc – *Maison Blanc*, Willen Field Rd, London NW10 7BQ and branches.

pp74–5: Teacloth and napkins, tea set, glass tazza, silver teaspoons – *The Dining Room Shop*, as above. Cushions and lavender bag – *Tobias and the Angel*, White Hart Ln, London SW13 OPZ.

pp76–9: Antique Indian picnic rug, French table linen, tapestry cushions, striped cushions (on chairs), backgammon set – *Guinevere*, as above. Antique French plates, bowl, wine basket, striped cushion (on rug), blue checked fabric, terracotta jug – *Nicole Fabre*, 592 Kings Rd, London SW6

2DX. Antique French knives, skittles, green glass bottle and jar – *Woodpigeon*, 71 Webbs Rd, London SW11 6SD. Antique baskets, bottle box, clear bottle, earthenware pot with cork lid – *Pimpernel & Partners*, 596 Kings Rd, London SW6 2DX. Antique linen cushions – *Braemar Antiques*, as above. French brasserie chairs – *House Points*, 48 Webbs Rd, London SW11 6SF.

pp80–1: Engraved silver gallery tray c.1860 – *Guinevere*, as above. Glasses, ice-bucket – *Annabel Elliot at Talisman*, Gillingham, Dorset, tel. 01747-824222.

pp82–5: Embroidered runner, napkins, tea service, milk jug, gold and white cake plate, knives – *The Dining Room Shop*, as above. Orange silk throw – *The General Trading Company*, as above. Glass plate and jam compote – *William Yeoward*, as above.

pp94–9: Antique antler candelabra, bronze stag, horn-handled cutlery, horn-and-silver sugar shaker, silver-rimmed horn beakers, silver-mounted light horn jug – *Guinevere*, as above. Contemporary antler salt and pepper shakers, horn salt dish and spoon, horn beakers, pair of horn utensil pots, horn dishes – *The General Trading Company*, as above.

pp100–3: Antique Scottish paisley shawl, late 19th-century Continental ruby cut-glass decanter, cigarette box, Sheffield plate basket c.1800, wine cooler, knives and forks, conch shells, plates – *Guinevere*, as above. Coffee cup and saucer – *The General Trading Company*, as before. Place-mats, mother-of-pearl hearts, silk purses – *Graham & Green*, 4, 7 & 10 Elgin Crescent, London W11 2JA. Silk-ribbon flowers – *V V Rouleaux*, 10 Symons St, London SW3 2TJ. Large chocolate heart – *Charbonnel et Walker*, One The Royal Arcade, 28 Old Bond St, London W1X 4BT (mail-order available). Truffles – *Maison Blanc*, as above.

pp104–11: Egg-and-feather china and napkins – *The General Trading Company*, as above. China Easter bonnet and baskets, miniature porcelain urns – *Annabel Elliot at Talisman*, as above. Painted and marble eggs – *Tobias and the Angel*, as above. Ornamental speckled eggs – *Damask*, 3 & 4 Broxholme House, 24 New Kings Rd, London SW6 4AA. Tassels, velvet flowers, stripey ribbon with spotted feather – *V V Rouleaux*, as above. Lemon cakes, apple and pear liqueur chocolates – *Maison Blanc*, as above.

pp112–15: Physalis rings, cinnamon-stick bundles, miniature tin watering can, throw and cushions (on sofa), tablecloths, napkins, plates – *The Conran Shop*, as above. Glass drop lantern, iron candelabras – *The General Trading Company*, as above. Glazed terracotta bowl, limestone bowls and platter, gnarled wooden dish and breadboard, wire basket, blue lantern – *Summerill & Bishop*, 100 Portland Rd, London W11 4LN. Multi-wick candle, night-lights and tea-lights – *Price's Candles*, 110 York Rd, London SW11 3RU.

pp116–23: Candlesticks, obelisks, goblets, china, tablecloth – *Annabel Elliot at Talisman*, as above. All candles (except beeswax) – *Price's Candles*, as above. Orange ribbons on napkins – *V V Rouleaux*, as above.

pp125–31: Antique round tablecloth and napkins, witch's balls, mercury-glass grapes, cut-glass candelabra (p125) – *Guinevere*, as above. Antique dinner plates and soup plates, wine goblets and finger-bowls, propaline lustre candelabras, glass salt cellars, contemporary tumblers – *The Dining Room Shop*, as above. Flatware – *Ever Trading*, as above. Painted metal toys, velvet roses, faux berries, silverplated fruit bowl – *Gisela Graham*, 12 Colworth Grove, Browning St, London SE17 1LR. Antique baubles on willow branches, baubles made from antique fabric (pp127 and 129), pomanders – *Tobias and the Angel*, as above. Velvet ribbon – *V V Rouleaux*, as above. Confectionery (p127) – *The Conran Shop*, as above.

DIRECTORY

(TL = top left; TR = top right; BL = bottom left; BR = bottom right; B = bottom; T = top; R = right)

China: p134: (TR) Marie Laage/Limoges – *Graham & Green*, as above. **(BL)** The Dining Room Collection – *The Dining Room Shop*, as above. **(BR)** The Blue Room/Spode – *The Dining Room Shop*, as above. **p135: (TL)** Chaine d'Ancre/Frédéric Dumas. **(TR)** The Cabinet Room Collection/Spode – *Peter Jones*, Sloane Sq, London SW1W 8EL. **(BL)** Scandinavian glazed plates – *The Dining Room Shop*, as above; Scandinavian glazed bowl – *The Blue Door*, 77 Church Rd, London SW13

9HH. **p136: (TL)** Marie Laage/Limoges – *Graham & Green*, as above. **(B)** *Wedding List Services*, 127 Queenstown Rd, London SW8 3RH. **p137: (TL)** Scandinavian dishes, knive and fork – *The Blue Door*, as above. **(TR)** Rupert Spira bowls and plates – *David Mellor*, 4 Sloane Sq, London SW1W 8EE. **(BL)** Comma/Peter Ting – *Thomas Goode & Co*, as above. **(BR)** Guilloche – *Thomas Goode & Co*, as above. **p138–9:** *Renwick & Clarke*, 190 Ebury St, London SW1W 8UP.

Glassware: p140–1: *William Yeoward*, as above. **p142: (TL)** Jubilant Platinum/Moser – *Thomas Goode & Co*, as above. **(TR)** Thistle/St Louis – *Thomas Goode & Co*, as above. **(BL)** Harcourt/Baccarat – *Thomas Goode & Co*, as above. **(BR)** Paula/Moser - *Thomas Goode & Co*, as above. **p143: (TL)** Coloured hock – *General Trading Company*, as above. **(BL)** Cranberry glass – *Dining Room Shop*, as above. **(BR)** Striped tumblers – *General Trading Company*, as above. **p144: (TR)** Salviati – *Thomas Goode & Co*, as above. **(B)** Carlo Moretti Calici Collection – *Thomas Goode & Co*, as above. **p145: (L)** Salir – *Thomas Goode & Co*, as above. **(TR)** Myrtle/William Yeoward – *Thomas Goode & Co*, as above. **(BR)** Alexandra/A Potter – *Thomas Goode & Co*, as above.

Flatware: p146: (TL) Gilt cutlery – *Wedding List Services*, as above. **(BL)** Enamelled coffee spoons – *Thomas Goode & Co*, as above. **(BR)** Kings Royal – *Peter Jones*, as above. **p147: (TL)** *Thomas Goode & Co*, as above. **(BL)** Pride – *David Mellor*, as above. **(R)** Avant Garde/Berndorf – *Thomas Goode & Co*, as above.

Table Linen: p148: (TR) White damask cloth and napkins – *The White Company*, 298–300 Munster Rd, London SW6 6BH. **(BR)** Linen table-mat and napkin, salt and pepper shakers, painted glass – *Maryse Boxer*, as above; cutlery, dish and spoons – *Thomas Goode & Co*, as above; plate – *Guinevere*, as above. **p149: (TL)** Royal Doulton. **(TR)** *The Hambledon Gallery*, 40–44 Salisbury St, Blandford, Dorset DT11 7PR. Mail-order available. **(BL)** Oriental silk runner and place-mat – *The General Trading Company*, as above; white linen tablecloth – *The Blue Door*, as above. **p150: (TL)** Napkin rings – *Graham & Green*, as above. **(TR)** Napkin with glass dots, *The Conran Shop* – as above; napkin rings – *Thomas Goode & Co*, as above. **(BL)** Napkin rings – *Thomas Goode & Co*, as above; napkins – *The Conran Shop*, as above; tablecloth – *Guinevere*. **(BR)** Silver napkin rings, linen napkin – *The Blue Door*, as above. **p151: (TR)** from top: *The Conran Shop, The Blue Door, Graham & Green, The Blue Door, The Dining Room Shop, Graham & Green*, all as above. **(BL)** Mother-of-pearl napkin rings – *The Dining Room Shop*, as above; linen napkins – *The Conran Shop*, as above; linen tablecloth – *Graham & Green*, as above. **(BR)** Napkin – *The Conran Shop*, as above; ribbon – *The General Trading Company*, as above; tablecloth – *The Blue Door*, as above.

Place Cards: p152: (TL) *The Dining Room Shop*, as above. **(TR)** Antique-fabric basket – *Tobias and the Angel*, as above; sugared chocolate pebbles – *Rococo*, as above. **(BL)** Hand-made antique-fabric decoration – *Tobias and the Angel*, as above. **(BR)** *The General Trading Company*, as above. **p153: (TR)** Sugar grapes – *Rococo*. **(BL)** Hand-made antique-fabric decoration – *Tobias and the Angel*, as above. **(BR)** *The Dining Room Shop*, as above.

Flowers: p154: (TR) Wire basket – *The Blue Door*, as above. **(BL)** Glazed dish – *The Dining Room Shop*, as above. **p155: (TL and TR)** Moulded-glass vases – *HRW Antiques*, 26 Sulivan Rd, London SW6 3DX. **(BL)** Glass vase – *The Conran Shop*, as above. **(BR)** Bowl – *HRW Antiques*, as above.

Candles: p156: (TL) Beeswax candle – *The Conran Shop*, as above. **(TR)** Glass-goblet and multi-wick candles – *The Conran Shop*, as above. **(BL)** Floating candles, bowl – *The Conran Shop*, as above. **(BR)** Cone-shaped candles – *The Conran Shop*, as above. **p157: (TR)** Candle shades – *Thomas Goode & Co*, as above. **(BL)** Glass twist candlesticks – *William Yeoward*, as above; twist candles – *Thomas Goode & Co*, as above. **(BR)** Miniature silver candlesticks – *Peter Jones*, as above.